An all original example of a Series VIII "German Child." See pages 184 and 185 for details.

Doll Classics

by Jan Foulke
Photographs by Howard Foulke

Published by HOBBY HOUSE PRESS, INC.
Cumberland, Maryland 21502

Printed in the United States of America
ISBN: 0-87588-298-6

Table of Contents

Acknowledgements

Again we would like to acknowledge and thank these friends, both collectors and dealers, whose dolls were photographed for use in the *Blue Books of Dolls & Values*, Volumes 1-4 and those whose dolls were specially photographed for the color sections in this volume. Through generosity such as theirs, doll knowledge can be shared as individual dolls are made available for study. It is to all of these named people, and in addition those who wished to remain anonymous, that we dedicate this book of *Doll Classics*.

Joanna Ott
Joyce Alderson
Pearl D. Morley
Grace Dyar
Thelma Bateman
Louise Ceglia
Emily Manning
Carole Stoessel Zvonar
Mary Lou Rubright
Elizabeth McIntyre
Richard Wright
Becky Roberts Lowe
Nancy Schwartz Blaisure
Clendenien Collection
Sheila Needle

Roberts Collection
Elizabeth Kennedy
Beth Foulke
Rosemary Dent
Glenn Mandeville
Crandall Collection
Mary Goolsby
Anarene Barr
Brand Collection
Gladyse Hills Hilsdorf
M. Elaine Buser
Jimmy & Faye Rodolfos
Esther Schwartz
Kay & Wayne Jensen

Coleman Collection
Carter Craft Dollhouse
Ann Tardie
Maxine Salaman
Chip Barkel
India Stoessel
T & H Antiques
Richard Saxman
Ruth Noden
Sue Bear
Anne W.
Carol Green
Betty Harms
Mike White

Introduction

Our *Blue Books of Dolls & Values* Volumes 1, 2 and 3 are history. Now out of print, they are available only on the secondary market where Volumes 1 and 2 are bringing what seem to us astonishingly, yet flatteringly, high prices. Since Hobby House Press, Inc., has received numerous requests for these early volumes, Gary Ruddell asked us to make a compilation of photographs from these first *Blue Books*. Hobby House Press, Inc. layout artists have reworked most of the photographs into a larger format than is possible to use in the *Blue Books* which impose severe size restrictions.

In reorganizing the photographs for this new volume, we have presented a pictorial overview of the antique and collectible doll field with chapters covering early wooden dolls through American compositions. These black and white photographs are taken from Volumes 1-4 with a few from Volume 5 where a series needed to be filled out. As a bonus, we have included nearly 100 of Howard's color photographs which have never appeared in any of our *Blue Books*. For each chapter, Jan has written introductions giving manufacturing and collecting information in more detail than can be covered within the limited confines of the *Blue Books* and fitting each type of doll into the historical framework of doll making. Since the emphasis of this book is on larger photographs, there was insufficient space for including drawings and illustrations of doll marks. The reader may consult the latest issue of the *Blue Book of Dolls & Values* for these.

I. French Bisque Dolls

Porcelain doll heads were apparently an invention of the German factories. First made in 1750 of china, a glazed porcelain, they did not become widely produced items until about 1840. By 1860, the china doll was beginning to loose favor to the bisque doll, another essentially German development, but this one brought to perfection by the finesse of the French manufacturers. Bisque is a high-fired translucent ceramic, unglazed or nonglossy. It is white and must be tinted to color.

Bisque doll heads were made in a two-part plaster mold with the seam line going down the side of the doll's head. Each working mold made from the master mold was used for producing about 50 heads. The first ones made from the mold had the sharpest features because the plaster wore down during many pressings.

The production of bisque involves a very complicated manufacturing process which must be carried out by skilled craftsmen at each of its many tedious steps to insure a top quality final product. Its essential ingredient is kaolin, a fine white clay, which, with addition of other substances such as quartz and feldspar, makes the porcelain slip which is placed into the molds to produce the heads. Actually at first, the bisque was rolled out, then pressed into the mold, leaving a rough finish on the inside, but by about 1870 in Germany, a process was developed to allow the bisque slip to be poured into the molds and at least some German heads were poured this early. The French, however, did not pour heads until 1890; however, by that date most German and French heads were poured. This new process was an important simplification in bisque production, as it required less time to simply pour the liquid porcelain into the plaster mold, instead of having to roll it out and pat it in by hand.

After a few minutes, when a layer of porcelain had adhered to the mold, the excess slip was poured off. After the clay had partially hardened and the head was removed from the mold, but before it was completely dry, any necessary cutting for openings in the bisque was done. These would be for eye and mouth openings, molded teeth, pierced ears and any openings necessary in the back of the head to accommodate mechanical devices. At this point also, the head was cleaned and smoothed to remove any mold debris or extra clay and prepared for the first firing. The high heat of this step hardened the clay. Next, the head was sanded, a very important step in producing smooth bisque. Then it was painted, first with an overall pink complexion coat, and after that had dried, the features — eyebrows, eyelashes, lips, cheek color and eyelid tinting — were added. Then the head was fired for the second time, but not at such a high temperature.

Some porcelain factories sold heads "in the white" to be decorated by purchasers. This was possible because the second firing, which set the decoration, could be accomplished at a much lower temperature than the first firing, which set the bisque.

Doll historians feel that some of the early French dolls had bisque heads which were produced in Germany as it appears that the Germans were likely producing bisque heads before the French were. In a review of the 1851 London Exhibition, the writer lamented that the French dolls heads could not compete with the pretty English faces or the "new porcelain heads made ... at Coburg or at Sonneberg." Another writer observed at this same Exhibition that very good porcelain heads, having been neglected by the French, were being produced in large numbers in Coburg, Sonneberg and Nürnberg. The backs of these heads were hollowed out so that the head would weigh less, as the duty was based upon weight, not numbers. These certainly sound like bisque or perhaps early china types made to have wigs.

In France, François Gaultier was producing excellent quality porcelain doll heads and parts in 1860 (He did not make complete dolls.), which he supplied to a large number of doll producers, including Gesland. It must be noted that few doll producers made their own heads as porcelain manufacture was a process requiring expensive kilns and highly skilled labor. It was much easier for them to buy heads from a porcelain factory and make their own bodies, wigs, and so forth. Casimir Bru started his business in 1866 and made complete dolls. Huret advertised bisque doll heads in 1865, but did not produce them. Jules Nicholas Steiner started his doll business in 1855; his line included early bisque dolls, and it appears that he made both heads and bodies.

Pierre Jumeau did not open his porcelain factory until 1873. Apparently before then he did purchase some heads in Germany, as an observer of the Vienna Exposition of 1873 reports: "M. Jumeau of Paris, the first and the most important doll-making house, has freed us from our former obligation to have the foreigner furnish us with porcelain doll heads." This is strange in the light of the fact that we know Gaultier,

Steiner and Bru were already producing their own bisque heads and parts. The Jumeau porcelain factory also supplied heads to other doll producers. Much more study needs to be undertaken on the French bisque doll manufacturers before the whole picture will become clear. It does seem, however, that in contrast to the German industry, where a few porcelain factories supplied most of the doll manufacturers and few producers made complete dolls, a larger portion of the French producers appear to have made both heads and bodies.

A. French Fashion Lady Dolls

In the 1850s, china, papier-mâché, and wax were popular media for doll heads, but in about 1860 the French lady doll with bisque head came into her own. These represented both adult and young ladies. The magazine *Harper's Bazar* did excellent and detailed reviews of the doll scene furnished from information supplied by prominent department and specialty stores. In 1867, the review noted a bisque head young lady doll with short brown curls and large braided chignon dressed as a miniature copy of a New York belle in a blue poplin dress. In 1868, the review observed that the French dolls with bisque heads were especially pretty with real blonde hair, deep blue eyes and plump cheeks. In 1869, dolls had real golden hair arranged in fancy styles, earrings and a velvet necklace concealing the neck joint which allowed the head to turn. A 12in (31cm) doll with bisque head and jointed arms and legs cost $15 undressed — indeed, a luxury at that time! In 1870, the review noted fine French dolls in sizes from 6in (15cm) to that of a child of three years. The heads turned and limbs were jointed. These cost $5 to $25 undressed. An outfit could be purchased for an additional $12.

The French lady dolls represented an overall quality product, which could not be matched by the Germans as far as bodies and clothing were concerned, although some of the early heads were possibly German imports. These ladies are referred to by collectors as *French Fashion* dolls or *Parisiennes* because of their lovely stylish clothing. The French dolls were always the best and most expensive. The last quarter of the 19th Century was an age of opulence and luxury which was reflected in the doll industry by the products of the French doll makers. They were noted not only for their beautiful dolls, but also for the outstanding outfits created by dressmakers as reflections of the latest fashions. These doll gowns were as elaborately presented as the originals, with luxurious fabrics such as silk, velvet, taffeta, satin and trimmings of braid, lace, ruffles, pleats, ribbons, buttons, drapes, and so forth. Some dresses are even replicas of the breathtaking ball gowns, such as those created by Worth and other couturiers. Many Paris toy shops specialized in making doll outfits which included everyday dresses, night wear, dinner dresses and ball gowns, as well as accessories such as boots, hats, purses, muffs, parasols, gloves, fans, underclothing — all sorts of items were available for the fashionable lady doll including jewelry such as brooches, watches and necklaces, and calling cards and writing sets. Lovely trunks

Illustration 1. François Gaultier made bisque heads and parts from 1860 to 1899, when he joined the S.F.B.J. group. According to research done by Mme. Poisson and presented in one of the CERP reports, Gaultier supplied heads for Gesland, Jullien, Petit & Dumontier, Rabery & Delphieu, Simonne, and Thuillier, among others. This lovely lady is incised on the shoulder with the F.G. initials. Thought to be an early model, she has painted eyes, an unusual feature for an F.G. doll. They are enhanced by long painted upper and lower eyelashes, and a dark stroke of eyeliner along the upper eyelid. She is 18in (46cm) tall. *Private Collection.*

9

could be purchased with inside compartments and shelves to hold all of "milady's treasures."

Of course, the lady dolls could also be purchased undressed. Patterns were available for dressing dolls at home, and this could be accomplished for less money than buying ready-made doll clothes. Wealthy homes often employed dressmakers on a regular basis, and sometimes they were commissioned to sew doll clothes from the scraps left from other garments. However, not all of the lady dolls were dressed in the latest Paris fashions. Some were clothed in regional costumes representing various French provinces. Most of these which have survived are of excellent workmanship with attention to authentic detail.

As far as collectors are concerned, the French lady dolls have not been overly popular; however, they are now beginning to attract attention. Perhaps the previous lack of widespread interest was because very few of them were marked with makers' names or labels, and it requires individual study in order to determine what to buy and how much to pay. Unmarked dolls require particular study, as they must be judged strictly on their own merits — chiefly beauty, quality and uniqueness; there is no delineated set of standards already established for them. Sometimes it takes courage on the part of a collector to make a purchase when there is no predetermined guide. Also, there are a variety of body types which can seem confusing to the beginner. It seems as though the French lady doll is surrounded by mystery because so little has been written about her, yet delving into her "mysteries" makes her more easily understood and a welcomed addition to a well-rounded or specialized doll collection.

Illustration 2. A beautiful F.G. fashion lady, 18in (46cm) tall. She has particularly large eyes and very heavy eyebrows for a Gaultier lady. Her upper lip, however, is fairly typical of F.G. ladies with two prominent upper peaks. *Mary Goolsby.*

Illustration 3. This large 24in (61cm) doll has the more typical F.G. lady look, with long narrow eyebrows consisting of tiny brush strokes and almond-shaped eyes outlined in black with lightly painted eyelashes. *Private Collection.*

OPPOSITE PAGE: Illustration 4. The Simonne establishment produced dolls from 1842 to 1881. At least some of their heads were purchased from Gaultier and Jumeau. Simonne dressed dolls and may have made doll bodies. Simonne lady dolls are stamped on the chest. This fine, marked example is 18in (46cm) tall, and is all original. *Sheila Needle Collection. Photograph by Morton Needle.*

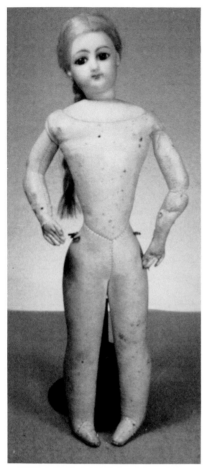 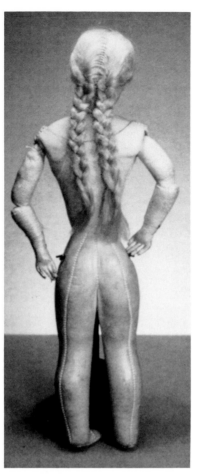

Illustration 7. Maison Huret was in business as early as 1812. In 1851 they advertised jointed dolls with porcelain heads. Huret lady dolls were produced with both bisque and china heads purchased from a porcelain factory. Huret apparently made bodies on which they placed their mark. Dolls had either painted or glass eyes. Huret was still in business as late as 1930. This early Huret doll has a rare face, referred to by collectors as a "Portrait Huret." 20in (51cm) tall, she is on a wood-jointed body with pewter hands and feet. *Richard Wright Collection.*

Illustrations 5 and 6. Head and shoulder plate by F. Gaultier on a typical French leather or kid body with gussets at elbows only. This would have been one of the less expensive bodies because there are no gussets at hips or knees, making a less desirable doll as she could not sit down. 12in (31cm) tall. *Carter Craft House Collection. Photograph by Thelma Bateman.*

LEFT and OPPOSITE PAGE: Illustrations 8 and 9. A beautiful French fashion lady, desirable not only for her lovely face, but also for her original, though tattered dress, much preferable to a replaced one. She wears a velvet choker to hide her neck joint and retains her original velvet hair band. She is outfitted with kid gloves, purse, bracelet and ring. 18in (46cm) tall, she has a bisque head, swivel neck and completely kid body. She is unmarked, as are the majority of French fashion ladies. *H&J Foulke, Inc.*

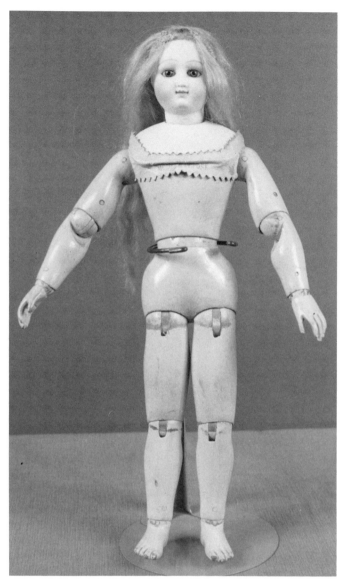

Illustration 10. Marked Bru fashion dolls as this one are fairly rare. She is incised on her shoulder "B. Jne et Cie." She is on the wooden fully-jointed body which Bru patented in 1869 with joints also at waist and ankles. She is 14in (36cm) tall. It has recently been discovered that the smiling fashion dolls which are marked with only a sizing letter A, B, C, and so forth were products of the Bru factory. *Dr. Carole Stoessel Zvonar Collection.*

TOP RIGHT: Illustration 11. This 16in (41cm) unmarked French fashion lady has a desirable face with moderately heavy eyebrows consisting of many very tiny brush strokes. She is redressed in an appropriate manner. *Mary Lou Rubright Collection.*

RIGHT: Illustration 12. This unmarked 18in (46cm) French lady wears her original dress which is over 100 years old. The design is fairly simple for the period, and could easily be copied for a doll lacking an appropriate costume. *Mary Goolsby.*

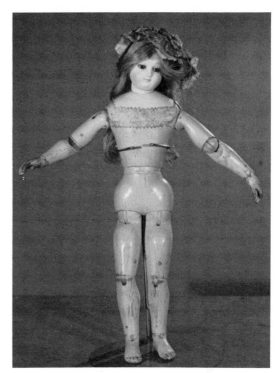

Illustration 13. Unmarked French fashion doll on a very desirable wood body, fully-jointed including waist and ankles. Shoulder, elbows, hips, knees and ankles are tenon joints; waist is a ball joint. A strip of kid covers the joining of the bisque shoulder plate to the wood body. She is 17in (43cm) tall. *Rosemary Dent Collection.* (See color photograph on page 17 for another wood jointed body.)

Illustrations 14 and 15. 18in (46cm) unmarked French fashion lady on a fully-jointed wood body, with an F.G. type face. Her very stylish outfit is green and white silk taffeta with black lace trim of the late 1870s. *H&J Foulke, Inc.*

LEFT: Illustration 16. Maison Jumeau was in the doll business as early as 1842, although he did not open his porcelain factory until 1873. Apparently before that time, he purchased heads from other makers and supplied his own bodies and clothing. The Jumeau fashion ladies are sometimes stamped on the bodies "JUMEAU//MEDAILLE D'OR//PARIS" in blue. Heads are marked only with a size number. This large Jumeau fashion lady marked on her body is 27in (69cm) tall, a rarely found size. *Mary Lou Rubright Collection.*

Illustration 18. A later type of lady made by Jumeau, probably after 1889, utilizing his Tête Jumeau head on a jointed composition body with adult proportions. The Tête head, which represents a child, seems strange on this body, but is perfectly proper. A further peculiarity about this doll is that although she has a lady body, her skirt is short as would be that of a child, although her bodice, hair and headdress would be appropriate for a lady. This example is 20in (51cm) tall. *Dr. Carole Stoessel Zvonar Collection.*

LEFT: Illustration 17. 22in (56cm) Jumeau fashion lady with head incised "E 7 J." Although it is unusual to find a marked E.J. head on a fashion body, this appears to be an original combination. The doll is wearing her original dress of the 1880s. *Private Collection.*

Continued on page 25.

The Gesland concern operated in Paris from 1860 until 1928. The firm made dolls, many of which had heads supplied by Francois Gaultier. Their most famous body was a wire frame shaped with cotton stuffing and covered with stockinette. When these bodies were used on fashion dolls, they included bisque hands and legs. The Gesland establishment also offered a complete doll repair service. The doll shown is 17in (43cm) tall and totally original. *Private Collection.*

LEFT: Mme Rohmer was in business making fashion dolls from 1857-1880, an early entrant into the fashion doll market. Many Rohmer dolls are stamped on the body. Heads are of china or bisque, with either stiff or jointed necks. Eyes can be either painted with eyelashes and dark upper eye line, or inset blown glass. Bodies are kid with bisque or china arms to match head. This doll is 17in (43cm) tall with bisque head and arms. As far as is known, Mme Rohmer purchased porcelain parts from a supplier and put them on bodies which she manufactured. *Private Collection.*

BOTTOM LEFT & RIGHT: This 15in (38cm) lady is unmarked, but she has a very beautiful face and a kid-over-wood-jointed body with bisque lower arms. *Private Collection.*

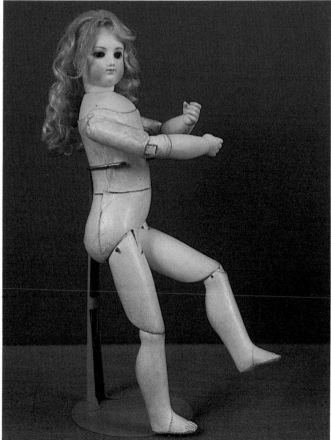

This 20in (51cm) French fashion lady has a very desirable face, although she has a stiff neck, whereas most collectors prefer a doll with a swivel neck. She is unmarked, but all original. *Private Collection.*

For more information on Jumeau dolls, see pages 26 to 30.

A 14½in (37cm) Portrait Jumeau with exceptional large and dark almond-shaped eyes. She is wearing a curly lamb's wool or fleece wig. *Private Collection.*

22in (56cm) doll with Jumeau head of the type usually found on lady kid bodies except this is on a jointed composition child body. Several of these have been found, but it is not known if the doll was ever originally offered with this combination. *Private Collection.*

A 20in (51cm) *Tête Jumeau* with closed mouth. *Joanna Ott Collection.*

A 17in (43cm) *Tête Jumeau* with closed mouth, all original. *Private Collection.*

A 21in (53cm) E.J. Jumeau with smooth creamy and pale bisque. *Private Collection.*

A 15in (38cm) incised Jumeau bébé. *Private Collection.*

An 18in (46cm) Francois Gaultier head incised with "F.G." block initials. *Joanna Ott Collection.* (For more information on Gaultier dolls, see page 8.)

A 26in (66cm) E.D. doll with closed mouth and unusually full auburn mohair wig. *Private Collection.* (For more information on E.D. dolls, see pages 33 and 34.)

20

A 17in (43cm) Figure C Series *Bébé Steiner*, all original. *Private Collection.* (For more information on Steiner dolls, see pages 36 to 40.)

A 13in (33cm) *Bébé Francais* marked "B.F." *Private Collection.* (For more information on B.F. dolls, see page 40.)

BELOW: A 13in (33cm) *Bébé Rabery* marked "R.D." *Private Collection.* (For more information on R.D. dolls, see page 42.)

CLOCKWISE: A 16in (41cm) unmarked French child of unknown manufacture. She has very desirable pale bisque, almond-shaped eyes and lamb's wool wig. *Private Collection.*

A 21in (53cm) unmarked French child with vivid skin tones, which appears to be made by Jumeau. *Private Collection.*

A 22in (56cm) early unmarked doll which is possibly an early Steiner. *Private Collection.*

A 16in (41cm) S.F.B.J. 251 character toddler. *Ruth Noden Collection.*

BOTTOM LEFT: A 15in (38cm) S.F.B.J. 238 smiling character girl. *Private Collection.*

BOTTOM RIGHT: A 13in (33cm) S.F.B.J. 227 character boy. *Private Collection.*

(See pages 47 to 49 for more information on S.F.B.J. character dolls.)

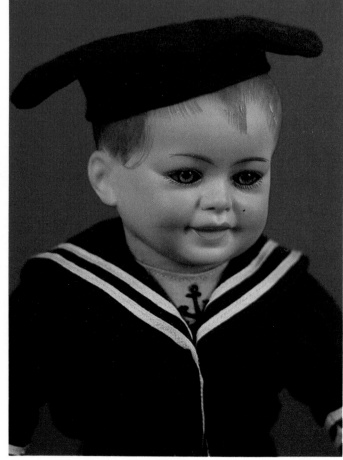

Continued from page 16.

CLOCKWISE: Illustration 19. Jumeau joined the French group S.F.B.J. (Société Française de Fabrication of Bébés & Jouets) which was formed in 1899 by various toy and doll makers to try to combat the increasing competition of the German companies. The bisque head of this lady doll carries the incised mark "S.F.B.J." with mold number "301" and a red Tête Jumeau stamp. She is on a fully-jointed composition lady body and measures 22in (56cm) in height. Many of these dolls had flirty eyes and real eyelashes. *Richard Wright Antiques.*

Illustration 20. S.F.B.J. continued producing the lady doll during the 1920 and 1930 period under the Unis trademark. This lady has the Unis 301 mold head on a shapely jointed composition body. Her costume in the Gibson Girl style shows off her molded bust and tiny waist. She is totally original. *H&J Foulke, Inc.*

Illustration 21. In the 1940s, Jumeau made a series of bisque head lady dolls from mold 221 representing various "Great Ladies in History." There were at least eight models: Mme. de Pompadour, Mme. de Sévigné, Marie Antoinette, Marie Louise, Queen Victoria, Josephine, Eugénie and Sarah Bernhardt. The dolls had glass eyes, fancy mohair wigs, and adult faces with closed mouths. The composition bodies were of five pieces with painted black slippers and a metal stand attached to the foot. All were dressed in fancy costumes with a paper Jumeau wrist tag. The dolls are 10-11in (25-28cm). Their original price was $15 each. *H&J Foulke, Inc.*

B. French Child Dolls

Certainly one of the greatest French innovations relating to the bisque head was the development of the bébé, the child doll. Jumeau claims to have designed the first bébé. He won his Gold Medal in 1878 for her, and all other manufacturers followed his lead. Lighter weight bodies in child proportions of papier-mâché and wood which were fully-jointed and maneuverable were designed for the new bébé. According to the Colemans, in 1879 Jumeau made 10,000 Bébés Jumeau, but by 1884 he was making 220,000 of them per year. Obviously, it did not take long for the new child doll to become all the rage and largely displace the lady dolls.

The French achieved their finest results in doll making with the bébés which were romanticized and idealized portraits of children. Indeed, François Theimer claims that a portrait of Henri IV as a young child was the model for the Bébé Jumeau head. The soul of the Bébé Jumeau is in her eyes. They seem to reach out and speak to the viewer. Certainly, Jumeau's makers per-fected the technique of the blown glass eyes of the paperweight type, which had a layer of clear glass over the eye to give depth and reality. The making of these eyes was a very exacting art and required a long period of apprenticeship. And when sometimes old dolls are found with eyes which are not exact matches in the diameter of pupil or iris, this is merely an indication of the fact that the eyes were all hand blown and that it was virtually impossible to get each one exactly like another. Because of the shape of the paperweight eyes, they were not adaptable to a weighted sleeping mechanism, so the French were fairly late in picking up the German innovation of sleeping eyes. Probably not until after 1900 do French dolls generally have sleeping eyes.

Certainly, the *Bébé Jumeau* was a pampered child. When factory dressed, she came in sumptuous outfits as elaborate as those made for the lady dolls, of the finest silks, satins and laces. (See color photograph on page 19 for an all original Jumeau child.)

Illustration 22. Probably the first *Bébé Jumeau* was the so-called Portrait or almond-eyed Jumeau. These dolls are stamped on the body "JUMEAU//MEDAILLE D'OR PARIS," but marked with only a size number on the head. The face is definitely related to that of the lady dolls, but with larger eyes and chubbier cheeks. Jumeau opened its own porcelain factory in 1873, so doubtless made most of these early bébés themselves. This wonderful Portrait Jumeau is a surprisingly small 11in (28cm) size. She has the early and very desirable fleece wig still attached to its skin base. She is totally original. *Richard Wright Collection.*

Illustration 23. This large 25in (64cm) Portrait Jumeau has outstanding almond-shaped eyes. There is white threading through the blue iris and a ring of darker blue around the outside. *Richard Wright Antiques.*

Illustration 24. The so-called Long-face or Triste is the most sought after Jumeau bébé. Her face is very distinctive, with the large luminous eyes, pensive, soulful or sad, which are a contributing factor to the "Jumeau Look." This model is marked on the head only with a size number. The early jointed wood and composition body is marked with a blue stamp "JUMEAU//MEDAILLE D'OR//PARIS." This particular doll is 24in (61cm) tall. *Private Collection.*

Illustration 25. This hauntingly beautiful Long-face is 30in (76cm) tall. She has the separately molded and applied ears which were used on the larger sizes of the pressed head dolls. *Crandall Collection.*

LEFT: Illustration 26. This lovely early doll is the very desirable E.J.//A. model. It is also marked on the body "JUMEAU//MEDAILLE D'OR//PARIS." This E.J.A. model is very rare, and seldom becomes available for purchase. This doll is 25in (64cm) tall. *Crandall Collection.*

27

CLOCKWISE: Illustration 27. A stunning doll is this 26in (66cm) doll incised "DÉPOSÉ// E 12 J." Her bright blue eyes and curly light blonde mohair wig complement her original navy blue coat and hat with light gold trim. She is totally original, including her bébé pin. *Private Collection.*

Illustration 28. The *Tête Jumeau* is the model which is found the most abundantly. She is stamped in red on the head "DÉPOSÉ// TÊTE JUMEAU//Bte SGDG" and on the body with the familiar blue stamp as above or oval paper sticker with "BÉBÉ JUMEAU//DIPLOME d'HONNEUR," the latter apparently a somewhat later mark. It appears that the *Tête Jumeau* model dates from about 1889, as the heads are made by the poured rather than pressed method. The doll pictured is 19in (48cm) tall, and is totally original. *Betty Harms Collection.*

Illustration 29. One type of Jumeau which was apparently made in a small edition, as it is difficult to find, is this face with the incised mark "JUMEAU//DÉPOSÉ." She seems to have smaller eyes than many of the E.J. and *Tête Jumeaux*. She is 15in (38cm) tall. *H&J Foulke, Inc.*

CLOCKWISE: **Illustration 30.** A 13in (33cm) *Tête Jumeau* with the typical pert face so appealing to collectors. *H&J Foulke, Inc.*

Illustration 31. A very appealing *Tête Jumeau* wearing a dress of about 1900. She is 19in (48cm) tall. *H&J Foulke, Inc.*

Illustration 32. Here is a 17in (43cm) red-stamped *Tête Jumeau* with an open mouth. Open-mouth dolls came onto the market in 1888, but in France they did not come into wide production until well into the 1890s. They are fairly plentiful in supply as Jumeau produced 3,000,000 dolls in 1897 alone! *H&J Foulke, Inc.*

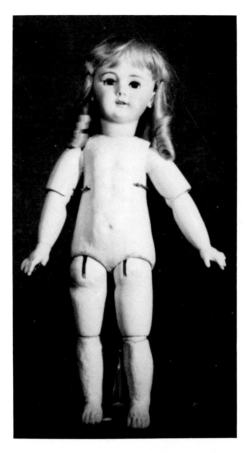

Illustration 33. Probably dating from after 1900, this doll is incised "DEP" with a red "TÊTE JUMEAU" stamp. Bodies of these dolls usually have the oval "BÉBÉ JUMEAU//DIPLOME d'HONNEUR" sticker. It is thought that these heads were made for Jumeau in Germany. Perhaps his own porcelain factory just could not keep up with the demand for Jumeau dolls. The dolls have sleeping eyes and real upper eyelashes with painted lower lashes. The mold is a distinctive one, easily recognizable and very popular with doll collectors. *H&J Foulke, Inc.*

Illustration 34. A very pert and appealing 13in (33cm) DEP, in a very attractive outfit of old clothing. *H&J Foulke, Inc.*

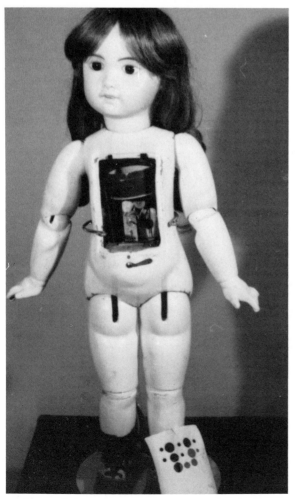

Illustrations 35 and 36. This is a 24in (61cm) *Bébé Jumeau Phonographe,* the doll that talked, laughed and sang. According to Constance King, she was first offered by Christmas 1893. In 1894, the Bon Marché Department Store advertised her for 52 francs, about $10, making her a fairly expensive doll. The phonograph dolls were apparently not very popular, as very few exist today. The doll illustrated has a Jumeau mold 230 character head (sometimes this same head is found marked "SFBJ 230"). The cavity in the torso accommodates a Lioret phonograph with wax cylinder, wound by a key protruding from the doll's back. *H&J Foulke, Inc.*
(See color photographs on pages 19 and 20 for additional Jumeau dolls.)

Illustration 37. The A.T. doll is one of the rarest of bébés; she was probably made by A. Thuillier. A.T. dolls are noted for their soulful eyes, softly painted eyebrows and quizzically painted mouth. They are the loveliest, most glamorous of dolls, with a very expressive countenance. Thuillier was in business from 1875 until 1890; his dolls are rarely found and very expensive. Some of Thuillier's heads were made by F. Gaultier. The smallest known A.T. is 9in (23cm) and the largest is 29in (74cm). The doll pictured is 22in (56cm) tall. *Mary Lou Rubright Collection.*

CLOCKWISE: Illustration 38. François Gaultier began making porcelain heads and parts and all-bisque dolls in 1860 and was in business until 1899, when he joined the S.F.B.J. Gaultier supplied various doll makers with heads, including Gesland, Jullien, Petit & Dumontier, Rabery & Delphieu, Simmone, and Thuillier, among others. Earlier bébés are incised with "F.G." in block letters separated by a size number; later dolls are incised "F.G." in a scroll. Of course, the earlier dolls are most desirable to collectors. This F.G. head is on a Gesland stockinette body. When used on child dolls, the Gesland body is accompanied by composition lower arms and legs and bisque shoulder plate. This doll is 14in (36cm) tall. *Richard Wright Antiques.*

Illustration 39. This doll is a 17in (43cm) incised "F.G." child with a very unusual face in that her cheeks are long, her eyes larger, and mouth painting different from most F.G. dolls. *Private Collection.*

Illustration 40. A very pretty "F.G." in scroll doll with vivid bright blue paperweight eyes. Her face is typical of dolls with this mark. *H&J Foulke, Inc.*

(See color photograph on page 20 for another F.G. doll.)

Illustration 42. Another beautiful *Paris Bébé*, this one is 32in (81cm) tall. *T & H Antiques.*

Illustration 41. The *Paris Bébé* trademark was registered by Danel & Cie in 1889, their first year of operation. They were in business until 1895, but their trademark was passed on through the S.F.B.J. *Paris Bébés* are well marked on both their bisque socket heads and jointed composition and wood bodies. According to François Theimer, Danel had been director of the Jumeau factory, but he left to begin his own business directly across the street. Jumeau successfully sued him because he had taken molds and tools from the Jumeau factory, lured away Jumeau workers and copied Jumeau heads and bodies. This doubtless explains why some of the *Paris Bébés* look like Jumeau dolls. (See *7th Blue Book of Dolls & Values*, page 306 for one that does.) The pictured doll is 25in (64cm) tall. *Richard Wright Antiques.*

Illustration 43. A very pretty doll incised "E.D." separated by size number "10," 17in (43cm) tall. M. Theimer has evidence which he feels indicates that Danel & Cie. made the dolls which are marked "E.D." *Mary Goolsby.*

TOP LEFT: Illustration 44. This 21in (53cm) E.D. doll is size 9. She has an open mouth with six molded upper teeth. (Most French open-mouth dolls have six teeth, German ones four.) Her clothes are appropriate replacements made from old fabrics. *H&J Foulke, Inc.* (See color photograph on page 20 for another E.D. doll.)

TOP RIGHT: Illustration 45. Bru dolls date from 1866 to 1899, when the company joined the S.F.B.J. The *Bébé Bru* certainly is a magical word in the French doll field. The earlier models on kid bodies are certainly among the most desired dolls today. The Bru concern made complete dolls; their quality control was high. Their bisque is generally very fine and delicately decorated. They had a large department which did nothing but dress dolls in the latest fashions made of the most luxurious and sumptuous fabrics. This 20in (51cm) doll with "BRU Jne" incised on her bisque head is wearing a totally original costume of the 1880s. *Richard Wright Collection.*

LEFT: Illustration 46. A large 30in (76cm) Bru Jne Bebe with lustrous vivid blue eyes, original soft mohair wig, and lips slightly parted to reveal the tip of her tongue. *Dr. Carole Stoessel Zvonar Collection.*

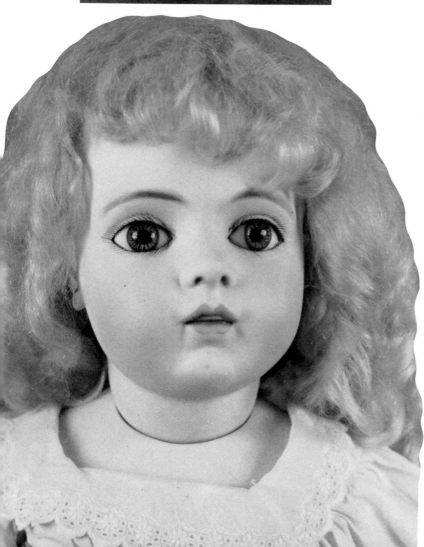

CLOCKWISE: Illustration 47. Bru made dolls in both mulatto shades like this 17in (43cm) tall bébé and darker black tones. (See *7th Blue Book of Dolls & Values*, page 87 for a black one.) This is an early model with parted lips and molded and painted teeth. Bru also made a doll with Oriental skin tones, which is the rarest of Bru models. *Richard Wright Collection.*

Illustration 48. Two undressed Bru dolls to show body structure. The left doll is a Bru Jne model with bisque head and shoulder plate with molded breasts, kid body, kid-over-wood upper arms, bisque lower arms, and carved wood lower legs. The doll on the right is a *Bébé Teteur* (Nursing Bru) with the original Bru rectangular paper label across her chest. *Thelma Bateman Collection. Photograph by Thelma Bateman.*

Illustration 49. A large 24in (61cm) *Bébé Teteur* patented in 1878, with a hole in her mouth to receive a nipple. A mechanism in her head sucks up liquid and operates by turning a key. The Bru concern was quite innovative and patented many doll inventions, such as a crying doll, a two-faced doll, a sleeping doll, an eating doll and a walking-talking doll. The illustrated doll has remains of her lamb's wool wig. She was designed to be a baby, even though she has the same body as the child doll. This, of course, predates the invention of the bent-limb baby body. During this period, a baby was signified by the clothing, not the body style. *Richard Wright Antiques.*

Illustration 50. Jules Nicholas Steiner started his business in 1855, and it went through various hands until 1908. Apparently Steiner had both a porcelain factory as well as a doll factory, so he made complete dolls and was an early entrant into the doll industry. Steiner dolls are not as plentiful as those made by Jumeau, and until recently had not been fully appreciated. But now there are dedicated collectors of the many varieties of Steiner dolls. Here is a 24in (61cm) Bourgoin Steiner of the C Series with moving eyes operated by a wire lever. The patent for this invention was granted in 1880. The iris and pupil are blown of glass and set into an opaque white eyeball. The eye mechanism inside the head is also marked "STEINER." Some Bourgoin Steiners have the caducous mark stamped on the body. *Richard Wright Antiques.*

RIGHT: Illustration 52. This 23in (58cm) Steiner doll is a Figure A Series girl with the 1889 Medaille D'or label of a girl carrying a flag on her body. She has particularly expressive eyes. The wide chubby cheeks and heavy eyebrows are typical of this series. *Joanna Ott Collection.*

OPPOSITE PAGE: Illustration 53. A lovely 24in (61cm) Figure A Series with a different look from the doll in *Illustration 52.* This one has a longer thinner face and feathery eyebrows composed of many individual strokes and is possibly an earlier model. *Richard Wright Antiques.*

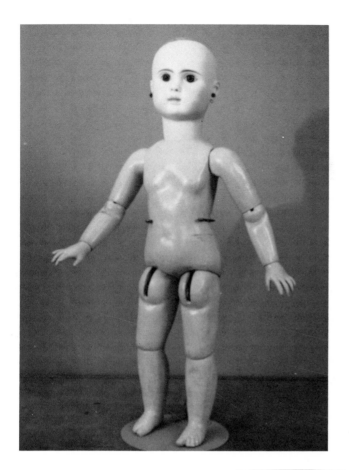

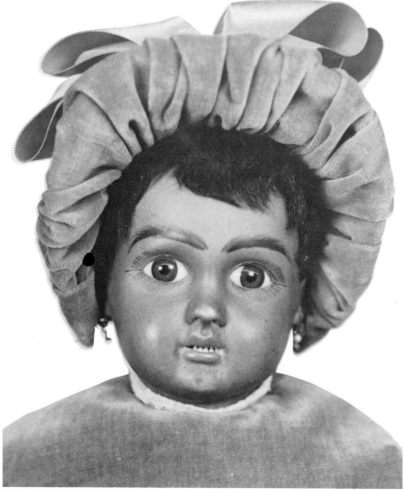

TOP LEFT and RIGHT: Illustrations 54 and 55. This is Steiner's *Bébé Le Parisien* from 1892. She is incised "A-19" (yet a different A Series) "PARIS" with a red stamp "LE PARISIEN." Her original body marked with a purple stamp, has long and graceful fingers, although the earlier Steiners often have short, stubby ones. She also has the separate and raised big toe typical of this period Steiner. Her purple cardboard pate is found exclusively on Steiner dolls. *Jan Foulke Collection.*

Illustration 56. Black French dolls are seldom found. Apparently, very few were made in comparison to the German porcelain factories which produced quite a few. This 18in (46cm) Steiner *Le Parisien* is incised "A-11." She has an open mouth with two rows of teeth. *Richard Wright Antiques.*

OPPOSITE PAGE: Illustration 57. A 19in (48cm) Steiner *Le Parisien* with open mouth and two rows of tiny teeth. Steiner was one of the few companies to use two rows of teeth in open-mouth dolls. *Mary Lou Rubright Collection.*

(See color photograph on page 21 for another Steiner doll.)

TOP LEFT: Illustration 58. The Schmitt firm was early into the doll business, 1854 until 1891. They apparently made both their heads and bodies. Their bisque head dolls are very desirable and difficult to find and are now bringing record prices. This 14in (36cm) *Bébé Schmitt* is marked with the crossed hammers in shield on both head and body. The bisque on the Schmitt dolls is of excellent quality with a pale complexion and delicate tinting. *Crandall Collection.* (See front cover for another Schmitt doll.)

LEFT: Illustration 59. The *Bébé Mascotte* trademark was owned by May Freres Cie, and later by the Société Steiner. Dolls were made from 1890 until 1901. Some of the heads look as though they might have been made by Jumeau, and some are on marked Jumeau bodies. The doll pictured is marked "MAS-COTTE" on the head; some dolls are marked on the body as well. It is 20in (51cm) tall. *Joanna Ott Collection.*

TOP RIGHT: Illustration 60. The *Bébé Français* trademark dates from 1891 and was used by Danel & Cie., Jumeau and the S.F.B.J. in that order. This doll appears to be an early 1890s model. She is marked "B.F." and is 26in (66cm) tall. *Richard Wright Antiques.* (See color photograph on page 22 for another B.F. doll.)

Illustration 61. This beautiful large 28in (71cm) French doll is marked "B.L." It is not certain who made this doll, though the Colemans now suggest that it may be *Bébé Lefebvre* made by Alexandre Lefebvre & Cie. *Private Collection.*

Illustration 63. This is a later open-mouth Jullien doll, marked "J J" (Jullien, Jeune). She is 15½in (39cm) tall. *Mary Goolsby.*

Illustration 62. Jullien owned a porcelain factory as early as 1827, but it is not known when he began to make doll heads; probably he was one of the early French doll makers. Jullien later joined the S.F.B.J. Jullien dolls are noted for their extremely heavy and glossy eyebrows. This marked Jullien doll is 19in (48cm) tall. *Richard Wright Antiques.*

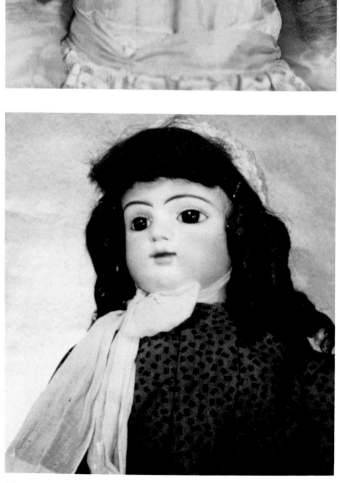

TOP LEFT: Illustration 64. One version of Roullet & Decamps *L'Intrêpide Bébé*, which has a French bisque head with closed mouth, possibly made by Jumeau. She is a mechanical doll with a key-wind walking body. *Richard Wright Antiques.*

LEFT: Illustration 65. Rabery & Delphieu were in the doll business as early as 1856. In 1899, they joined the S.F.B.J. They purchased at least some of their heads from François Gaultier. This closed-mouth doll marked "R.D." is 28in (71cm) tall. *Coleman Collection. Photograph by Thelma Bateman.*

TOP RIGHT: Illustration 66. A stunning all original 19in (48cm) R.D. *Anarene Barr Collection. Photograph courtesy of the owner.*

(See color photograph on page 22 for another R.D. doll.)

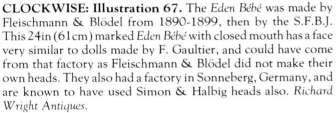

CLOCKWISE: Illustration 67. The *Eden Bébé* was made by Fleischmann & Blödel from 1890-1899, then by the S.F.B.J. This 24in (61cm) marked *Eden Bébé* with closed mouth has a face very similar to dolls made by F. Gaultier, and could have come from that factory as Fleischmann & Blödel did not make their own heads. They also had a factory in Sonneberg, Germany, and are known to have used Simon & Halbig heads also. *Richard Wright Antiques.*

Illustration 68. A very pretty 23in (58cm) doll marked "EDEN BÉBÉ//PARIS" on a walking composition jointed body. *H&J Foulke, Inc.*

Illustration 69. An *Eden Bébé* with open mouth and four rounded upper teeth. She has particularly lovely paperweight eyes, dark eyebrows with many individual strokes to shape the tops, and very long painted eyelashes. *Joanna Ott Collection.*

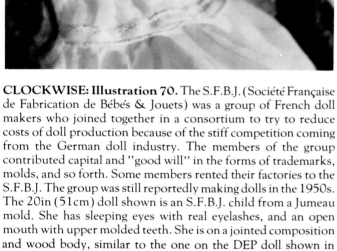

CLOCKWISE: Illustration 70. The S.F.B.J. (Société Française de Fabrication de Bébés & Jouets) was a group of French doll makers who joined together in a consortium to try to reduce costs of doll production because of the stiff competition coming from the German doll industry. The members of the group contributed capital and "good will" in the forms of trademarks, molds, and so forth. Some members rented their factories to the S.F.B.J. The group was still reportedly making dolls in the 1950s. The 20in (51cm) doll shown is an S.F.B.J. child from a Jumeau mold. She has sleeping eyes with real eyelashes, and an open mouth with upper molded teeth. She is on a jointed composition and wood body, similar to the one on the DEP doll shown in *Illustration 33. H&J Foulke, Inc.*

Illustration 71. This is a 29in (74cm) S.F.B.J. child, again from a Jumeau mold. She has the six molded upper teeth, typical of the early open-mouth French dolls. *H&J Foulke, Inc.*

Illustration 72. A 10in (25cm) S.F.B.J. child from mold 301. She has blue sleeping eyes with real eyelashes and open mouth with four upper teeth. She is on a jointed composition and wood body. She appears to be *Bleuette*, from *La Semaine de Suzette* which was a French magazine for young girls. She is all original and dates from about 1918. *H&J Foulke, Inc.*

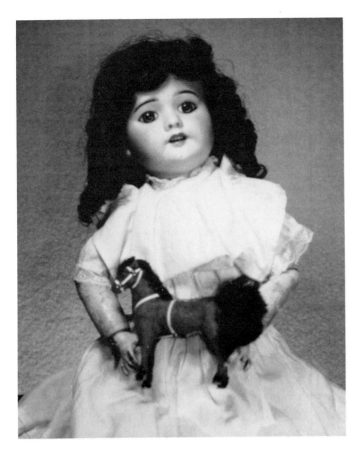

CLOCKWISE: **Illustration 73.** Here is a very pretty S.F.B.J. dolly face from mold 60. The S.F.B.J. dolls vary in quality and must be judged individually. Usually the 301 mold dolls are better quality than the 60 mold dolls, but there are exceptions as, of course, the heads were hand finished and painted. *Coleman Collection. Photograph by Thelma Bateman.*

Illustration 74. S.F.B.J. patented a flirty-eyed, walking, kiss-throwing doll in 1905. The composition body has straight legs. A mechanism inside the torso moves the head from side to side as the legs move. A pull string raises her hand to her mouth to throw a kiss. These dolls are very popular with collectors. This one carries the "UNIS" mark which S.F.B.J. used after 1916. She is 22in (56cm) tall. *Emily Manning Collection.*

Illustration 75. A very cute Unis 301 doll with a fully-jointed composition body, wearing original clothing. She is 12in (31cm) tall. *Becky Roberts Lowe.*

C. French Character Dolls

The Character Doll Movement of the early 1900s, which reached full proportions by 1909, was essentially a German development. The German factories produced unbelievably natural looking dolls which appeared to be portraits of real children. The French consortium S.F.B.J. was soon to follow the German lead and produce a series of character dolls. Saint-Denis adver-tised character dolls with molded hair and jointed composition bodies in their 1911 catalog. La Samaritaine in 1913 offered character dolls with wigs, but none appeared to have a bent-limb body. Apparently, the number of character dolls produced was only a small portion of total production, and the dolly face doll continued to be more important.

OPPOSITE PAGE: Illustration 76.
S.F.B.J. mold 226 appears to be their first character number and could be the doll shown in the 1911 Saint-Denis Catalog. It is a cute 13½in (34cm) boy with open/closed smiling mouth (no teeth) and bald head with painted hair. The painted hair on most of the S.F.B.J. characters is applied in streaks which often do not fully cover the scalp. He has inset glass eyes with painted eyelashes. He is on a jointed composition body. *Mary Lou Rubright Collection.*

Illustration 77. Here are two examples of S.F.B.J. mold 227. These have a smiling mouth with molded teeth and painted hair applied in individual strokes. They are about 14in (36cm) tall. *Richard Wright Collection.* (See color photograph on page 24 for another 227 doll.)

LEFT: Illustration 78. The "Screamer" is 14in (36cm) tall with small glass eyes and a very wide open/closed mouth. He is S.F.B.J. mold number 233, also on a jointed composition body. *Ruth Noden Collection.*

Illustration 79. This 15in (38cm) S.F.B.J. mold 236 character has an open/closed mouth with molded tongue and two upper teeth. He originally had real upper eyelashes which are now missing, and he has painted lower eyelashes. He is on a jointed composition toddler body with chunky limbs marked with an oval "SFBJ" sticker. This head also comes on a bent-limb baby body. *H&J Foulke, Inc.*

LEFT: Illustration 80. A rarely found doll is this S.F.B.J. mold number 234 character baby which has an open/closed mouth with molded tongue. She is 18in (46cm) tall on a bent-limb baby body. *Richard Wright Collection.*

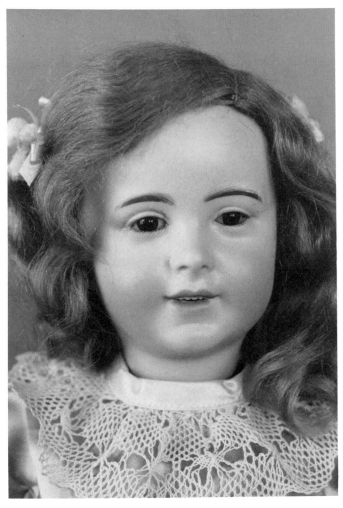

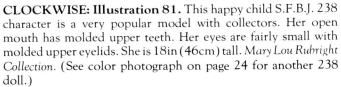

CLOCKWISE: Illustration 81. This happy child S.F.B.J. 238 character is a very popular model with collectors. Her open mouth has molded upper teeth. Her eyes are fairly small with molded upper eyelids. She is 18in (46cm) tall. *Mary Lou Rubright Collection.* (See color photograph on page 24 for another 238 doll.)

Illustration 82. This nice large 21in (53cm) baby is on a toddler body. She is S.F.B.J. mold 247, referred to as "Twerp." She has an open/closed mouth with two molded upper teeth, and an enchanting expression, which is popular with collectors. *Richard Wright Collection.*

Illustration 83. The most desirable and most expensive of the S.F.B.J. characters is this mold 252 pouty baby, which comes on both baby and toddler bodies. The pictured doll is a 26in (66cm) tall toddler. *Richard Wright Collection.*

II. German Bisque Dolls

Although the Chinese had known the secrets of porcelain making since before the year 1000 A.D., it was not until the early 1700s that a German chemist discovered the formula for hard paste transluscent porcelain. K.P.M., known familiarly as Meissen, was the first German factory to produce porcelain from this recipe. Two other Germans who developed porcelain recipes of their own around 1750 both became established in factories in the Thüringian forests. Porcelain soon became a very prosperous industry in the Sonneberg area.

Doll heads of porcelain were essentially an invention of the German doll industry. This is not surprising when one considers the history of the toy industry in the part of Germany known as Thüringia, which already had hundreds of years of toy-making tradition. By this time, Sonneberg and the surrounding area based its economy on the toy industry. Whole villages made their living producing toys. With Sonneberg an important center not only for the toy business, but also for the porcelain trade, it seemed only a natural blend for someone in the toy or porcelain trade to conceive the idea of making dolls and dolls' heads of porcelain. Everything was ripe in Thüringia for this type of doll making. There were forests in which to obtain wood to fuel the furnaces and to use in carving bodies and parts; there was the right kaolin for the porcelain to make the heads; there was plenty of cheap skilled and unskilled labor, as many facets of doll production were carried out as a cottage-type industry. The first porcelain heads were of china, a glazed or glossy porcelain. Although china head dolls were made as early as the mid-1700s, it was not until the 1840s that they began to be produced in greater numbers.

By 1860, the porcelain factories were making heads of unglazed porcelain which is called bisque. Primarily, the early bisque heads were of the shoulder type with molded hairdos. But soon the German factories were copying the French fashion ladies, producing dolls with swivel necks on bisque shoulder plates with kid or cloth bodies. By the late 1870s, they were copying the French Bébés, having been quick to see the success of the French child doll. Indeed, there is a Jumeau doll in one of the German museums today which is said to have been brought home by one of the German makers from a trip to Paris.

Competition became very keen between France and Germany, but the Germans opted for what they could do best — produce a large quantity of dolls cheaply. They left the luxury up to the French and produced the basic dolls. For the next 30 years, the Germans were primarily producing copies of French dolls. But with their vast natural resources and cheap labor, they could produce and sell their products at a much lower price than the French could. Many German dolls were just as fine as the French ones, but, of course, many were not. The French produced the luxury dolls; the Germans made the bread and butter dolls, but in so doing the Germans developed a thriving and very profitable trade. Indeed, the German doll factories produced a dynasty of interrelated families and generations living in palatial residences.

Many of the first German bisque doll heads are known to have been made by factories of Kling & Co., Alt, Beck & Gottschalck, Simon & Halbig, and probably J.D. Kestner, all of the Waltershausen/Ohrdruf area. The porcelain factories making bisque doll heads in Sonneberg did not begin until the 1880s. Apparently for the 15 to 20 years before 1880, production was concentrated over the mountains in the Waltershausen/Ohrdruf area of Thüringia, where Kestner was the first to establish his doll factory. With his prosperity, other doll factories followed in Waltershausen and with Kestner's purchase of a porcelain factory in 1860, he was apparently one of the pioneers of the bisque doll head.

This new development of bisque heads gave great momentum to the German doll industry. Although eventually millions of bisque doll heads came out of the Sonneberg factories, it was the Ohrdruf area which produced the finest grade of bisque. Their heads became known around the world for fine quality. Even some of the French makers used bisque heads from this area.

It should be noted that very few factories made both heads and bodies. Most heads were made by porcelain factories who supplied more than one doll factory. Following is a list of porcelain factories. As far as is known, only J.D. Kestner, A. Schoenau, A. Marseille, H. Steiner and Max Oscar Arnold had both doll factories and porcelain factories so that they could produce a complete doll. Of course, there were also many smaller porcelain factories in Germany who produced doll heads as a side line (particularly china heads) which have not been identified.

Ohrdruf Area Porcelain Factories
Simon & Halbig (1869)
Alt, Beck & Gottschalck (1854)
Bähr & Pröschild (1871)
Kling & Co. (1834)
Hertel, Schwab & Co. (1910)
Schützmeister & Quendt (1889)
J.D. Kestner (1816 dolls, 1860 porcelain)
Sonneberg Area Porcelain Factories
Recknagle (1886)
Swaine & Co. (1910 for dolls)
Ernst Heubach (1887)
Gebrüder Kühnlenz (1884)

Porzellanfabrik Mengersgereuth (1908)
Limbach (1883 for novelties)
Max Oscar Arnold (1887)
Gebrüder Knoch (1887)
Goebel (1887 dolls)
Schoenau & Hoffmeister (1884 dolls, 1901 porcelain)
Armand Marseille (1884 dolls and porcelain)
Hermann Steiner (1909 dolls and porcelain)
Porzellanfabrik Rauenstein (1892)
Lichte Area Porcelain Factories
Gebrüder Heubach (1910 dolls)
Hertwig (1884 dolls)

A. German Bisque Lady Dolls

LEFT: Illustration 84. The early bisque shoulder head dolls with molded hair of the 1860s which have no flesh tinting are referred to as Parian-type dolls; mostly these are lady dolls; only a few are children. Unfortunately, most of them are unmarked, so it is not known which factories created these lovely dolls. This beautiful Parian-type lady is a wonderful example of the German doll makers' art. Her hair is molded in fancy upswept style with separately applied hair bow; her hairline was delicately painted with tiny brush strokes which give a realistic look. She has pierced-in ears to accommodate earrings. A very desirable feature is the decoration of her shoulder plate with separately applied porcelain ribbons and flowers. Most embellished shoulder plates are decorated with gold or pink lustre trim. She is 18in (46cm) tall. *Private Collection.*

Illustration 85. This 21in (53cm) lady is another lovely Parian-type. She has pale blue painted eyes, tinted cheeks and fancy molded blonde hair with molded flowers for decoration. Another desirable feature is her molded necklace. *Grace Dyar.*

Illustration 86. This Parian-type doll has blonde molded hair combed back from her face and held with a black molded and painted ribbon. Collectors refer to this style as "Alice" (as in Wonderland), but this doll appears to be more a young lady than a child. *Richard Wright Antiques.*

Illustration 87. This beautiful 17in (43cm) lady with glossy blonde molded hair has lovely painted eyes with a two-color iris and white dot highlights. Her pierced ears to accommodate earrings are a desirable feature. *Mary Goolsby.*

Illustration 88. A lady with light brown hair in a less elaborate coiffure. She is wearing a molded white blouse with scarf trimmed in lustre. She is 17½in (45cm) tall. *Mary Goolsby.*

Illustration 89. This 19in (48cm) Parian-type lady has a hairdo which is often found on china head dolls. Although this doll has superior molding details, even showing comb marks on her curls, her outstanding feature is her glass inset eyes with tiny painted eyelashes. She dates from the 1860s. *Joyce Alderson Collection.* (See color photographs on pages 57 and 58 for additional examples of early dolls with molded hair.)

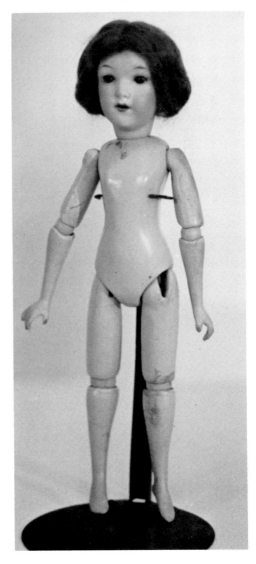

CLOCKWISE: **Illustration 90.** Most of the bisque dolls with molded headwear date from about 1890 to 1910. The quality varies and the price runs accordingly. They do not have the same fine bisque and delicate decoration as the early Parian-type dolls, but are attractive in their own way. This blonde-haired bisque doll with molded tam is 16in (41cm) tall and of nice quality. *Private Collection.*

Illustration 91. A 15in (38cm) bisque doll with a nicely molded hat simulating a straw bonnet with flower decoration in relief on the upturned brim. *Mike White Collection.*

Illustration 92. Lady dolls became popular again in 1910. The 12 to 14in (31 to 36cm) lady dolls have very slim bodies as this example which is an Armand Marseille 401 mold with open mouth. The feet were molded to wear high-heeled shoes; the bust is de-emphasized. These slender bodies were offered as late as 1930 by Montgomery Ward. Collectors refer to these as flapper bodies. *Mike White Collection.*

LEFT: Illustration 93. A 13in (33cm) A.M. 401 lady with open mouth, all original costume, flapper body, post World War I. *Mike White Collection.*

Illustration 94. Simon & Halbig also made heads for lady dolls. This attractive lady with a closed mouth and sleeping eyes was made by S & H for Cuno & Otto Dressel from mold 1469. This is a fairly difficult doll to find. She has a slim body like the A.M. doll in *Illustration 92.* She is wearing her original ribbon and lace-trimmed teddy. She is 12in (31cm) tall. *Mike White Collection.*

LEFT: Illustration 95. The most easily found lady doll is Simon & Halbig's model 1159 which was registered in 1894. This is an open-mouth doll with glass sleeping eyes and a slender adult face. Her molded eyebrows are painted with delicate individual strokes. She has painted upper and lower eyelashes, although some examples of this model have real upper lashes instead of painted ones. She has pierced ears to accommodate earrings. Her body has a molded bust, slim waist and slender arms and legs. Because of her body style, she is a popular doll with collectors. This 14in (36cm) Simon & Halbig 1159 has the slender flapper body like the A.M. doll in *Illustration 92.* She is all original in a blue silk 1920s dress and cloche hat. *H&J Foulke, Inc.*

54

Illustration 96. One of the most popular and sought after of the German lady dolls is Kestner's *Gibson Girl*, which dates from 1910. This bisque shoulder head doll sometimes is marked with mold number 172. She is on a rivet-jointed kid body which sometimes has the name *Gibson Girl* stamped in blue on the torso and usually has the Kestner paper crown and streamers label. The *Gibson Girl* has an oval face with delicate features; the upward tilt of her chin gives her a haughty look. She has an enigmatic smile which emphasizes her high cheek bones. This lady is 21in (53cm) tall. *Mary Lou Rubright Collection.*

OPPOSITE PAGE: A beautiful bisque lady with blonde molded hair in a fancy style with a fall down the back of her neck. A blue hair ribbon with lustre trim is tied around her head. She has pierced ears and inset blue glass eyes. Altogether a very lovely and desirable doll, she is wearing her original blue plaid dress. *Private Collection.*

Illustration 97. This stunning Simon & Halbig character lady is mold 1303, a rare doll to find. Her closed lips are thin and wide, softly closed and delicately painted with extra shading lines, the upper one slightly bowed. Her molded eyebrows are set close to her eye socket and are painted with long delicate brush strokes. She has no molded upper eyelid, but is intended to have real eyelashes. Her ears are pierced for earrings. She is 18in (46cm) tall. *Richard Wright Collection.*

Illustration 98. This is a particularly lovely example of the smallest size *Gibson Girl,* only 10in (25cm) tall. These dolls have painted lower lashes only, as they were intended to have real upper ones, although most often they have worn away. The eyebrows on this doll are painted with many individual strokes, although some *Gibson Girls* have long one-stroke eyebrows. *Becky Roberts Lowe.*

Continued on page 65.

56

This 19½in (50cm) German lady with swivel neck on a bisque shoulder plate is a wonderful example of a German fashion doll. It is the type of doll created to meet the challenge of the French fashion doll. Many of the German bisque dolls of the 1870s were as fine in quality as the French dolls, although their kid bodies were not as shapely or as well made as the French ones. She is unmarked. *Joanna Ott Collection.*

TOP LEFT: Another beautiful bisque head lady with molded blonde hair in an unusually high hairdo. She has pierced ears, blue glass eyes and is all original. Indeed, a very rare doll. *Private Collection.*

LEFT: This 23in (58cm) doll is unmarked, but there seems little doubt that she is from Simon & Halbig's mold 1388. Her upper eyelids are deeply molded and she has fringed eyelashes. Her flirty eyes move from side to side on a glass rod in her head. She is dressed in a maroon coat and hat; her wig is of white mohair. *Dr. Carole Stoessel Zvonar Collection.*

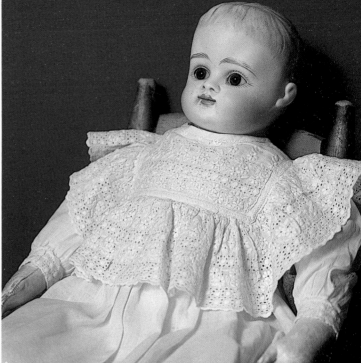

This 13in (33cm) boy has blonde molded hair and blue glass eyes. A lovely early doll, he is unmarked, but appears of Waltershausen/Ohrdruf quality. He is on a cloth body with leather arms and is wearing his original gown. *Anne W. Collection.*

LEFT: A 15in (38cm) Belton-type doll with bisque socket head and jointed composition body in an all original outfit. She could be of French or German manufacture. *Private Collection.*

A small 11in (28cm) doll with bisque head incised "275" by Bähr & Pröschild. She is all original, including her very full blonde mohair wig. *Private Collection.*

59

OPPOSITE PAGE: A large 32in (81cm) J.D.K mold 249 character girl, dating from 1915. She is a treasure in that not only is she a rarely found mold, but in a rarely found size. *Joanna Ott Collection.*

Two children by Simon & Halbig. Left is a 17in (43cm) girl from mold 939; right is a 15in (38cm) from mold 749. Both have open mouths and are on jointed composition bodies. *Mary Lou Rubright Collection.* (For other S & H dolls, see pages 70 to 73.)

BOTTOM LEFT: Here is a sweet 22in (56cm) child by the Schoenau & Hoffmeister porcelain factory, mold 5500. She is all original. *Anne W. Collection.* (For another Schoenau & Hoffmeister doll, see page 78.)

BELOW: A very rare 18in (46cm) Simon & Halbig mold 1302 black bisque character girl, whose face shows exceptional skill in the art of doll sculpting. The black dolls with Negroid features, as this one, are much more realistic than simple black or brown versions of Caucasian faces. This doll has a broad nose with flaring nostrils and indented philtrum. Her full red lips are closed, almost in a pouting expression. *Carol Green Collection.* (For other black dolls, see pages 84 to 87.)

CLOCKWISE: An 11in (28cm) J.D.K. 221 googly. These whimsical charmers with side-glancing eyes began to appear in 1911. Certainly, the influence of Rose O'Neill and Grace Drayton can be seen in the faces of these cuties. *Private Collection.* (For more information on Kestner character dolls, see pages 108 to 109.)

A 20in (51cm) K★R 114 character boy, all original evening outfit. *Private Collection.*

A 16in (41cm) K★R 101 character girl with glass eyes, a rarely found feature on this mold number. *Richard Wright Antiques.*

A 22in (56cm) K★R 107 rarely found character *Carl* dating from 1909. *Richard Wright Antiques.* (For more information on K★R character dolls, see pages 91 to 96.)

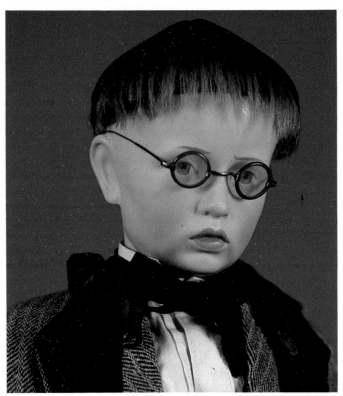

Another rare character girl incised only "128" with glass eyes, by an unknown maker. Her crown opening is very small, and she could have been made by the same factory as the "111" character. She is 20in (51cm) tall on a jointed composition body. *Richard Wright Collection.*

RIGHT: Mold 536 character girl with glass eyes made by Bähr & Pröschild for Kley & Hahn. *Esther Schwartz Collection.* (For more information about Kley & Hahn character children, see page 96.)

BELOW: A rare character girl incised only "111" with painted eyes, by an unknown maker. The crown opening is very small. This mold is also found with glass eyes. (See *Simon & Halbig Dolls,* page 157.) *Mary Lou Rubright Collection.*

A pair of toddlers made by Swaine & Co. porcelain factory. They illustrate two different treatments of the same mold, the girl having glass eyes and wig, the boy having molded hair and deep intaglio eyes. Both have excellent bisque and modeling. She is incised "DIP;" he is incised "DI." Both are size number 6 and have the round green stamp S & Co. *Kay & Wayne Jensen Collection.*

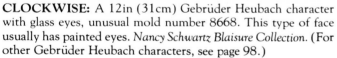

CLOCKWISE: A 12in (31cm) Gebrüder Heubach character with glass eyes, unusual mold number 8668. This type of face usually has painted eyes. *Nancy Schwartz Blaisure Collection.* (For other Gebrüder Heubach characters, see page 98.)

A 30in (76cm) Kämmer & Reinhardt 128 mold character baby, extremely rare in this large size. *H&J Foulke, Inc.* (For other Kämmer & Reinhardt characters, see pages 103 to 105.)

An 18in (46cm) rare character girl incised "BP" made by Swaine & Co. She has deep intaglio eyes and a wide smiling mouth with molded teeth. *Richard Wright Antiques.* (For more information about Swaine & Co. character dolls see page 114.)

Continued from page 56.

B. German Bisque Child Dolls

The bisque head child doll was a staple product of the German doll industry for nearly half a century. Though basically a French invention, it was the German dolly which dominated the market. The Germans did, however, due to their own ingenuity, add novelty to their wears by the invention of weighted sleeping eyes, flirty eyes and open mouths with molded or inserted teeth, as well as the use of real eyelashes and eyebrows. They also improved the flexibility of the jointed composition bodies and added voice boxes, walking mechanisms, multiple faces and other novelties.

Bachmann reports that German dolls accounted for two-thirds of the world market at the beginning of the 20th Century. The German factories produced a good doll at a very competitive price, much less than the French dolls. The Germans could do that because of their abundance of cheap labor and their low overhead. Whole families worked together at home — making shoes, clothing, wigs, body parts — then assembling the finished product.

The open-mouth doll showing teeth came onto the market in about 1888. The *Youth's Companion* for that year noted specifically that its premium doll had an open mouth and pearly porcelain teeth. *Ridley's Fashion Magazine* for winter 1888 offered a bisque head doll with open mouth and teeth. At first the price for the open-mouth doll was more expensive. By 1890, nearly all of the dolls had this new feature.

Waltershausen/Ohrdruf Area Dolls

Illustration 99. A group of three bisque shoulder head children with molded hair, all dating from the last quarter of the 19th Century. Left is a 12in (31cm) blonde-haired girl, so-called "Highland Mary" with painted blue eyes; many of these are from mold 1000 by Alt, Beck & Gottschalck. The center boy has blonde molded hair with side part and comb marks; his eyebrows are thick with many brush strokes and he has glass eyes; this head also was made as a socket head to be used on a jointed composition body. Right is a 15in (38cm) doll with short blonde hair and exposed ears; this appears to be mold 784 by Alt, Beck & Gottschalck, who also made this head in china. Although this head was probably intended to be a child, many collectors dress it as an adult. *Joanna Ott Collection and H&J Foulke, Inc.*

Illustration 100. A very nice example of a bisque shoulder head boy with molded hair and painted eyes, he is 15in (38cm) tall and incised "30/B2//Germany." The maker of these sweet boy dolls has not been determined, but they are fine quality and appear to be Waltershausen/Ohrdruf area dolls. *Brand Collection. Photograph by Thelma Bateman.*

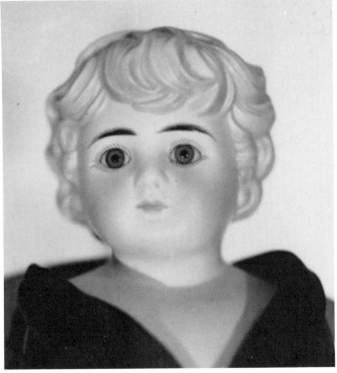

Illustration 101. A 17in (43cm) child with molded blonde hair and inset glass eyes appears to be mold 1288 by Alt, Beck & Gottschalck. These molded hair children were made in the 1880s. *Mary Goolsby.*

Illustration 102. A 16in (41cm) Parian-type child dressed as a boy. He has short molded curly blonde hair and inset blue glass eyes. The shoulder head has a very deep plate and is mounted on a cloth body with leather arms. He is all original. *Grace Dyar.*

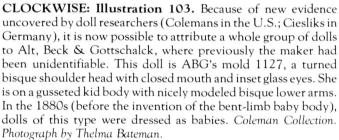

CLOCKWISE: Illustration 103. Because of new evidence uncovered by doll researchers (Colemans in the U.S.; Ciesliks in Germany), it is now possible to attribute a whole group of dolls to Alt, Beck & Gottschalck, where previously the maker had been unidentifiable. This doll is ABG's mold 1127, a turned bisque shoulder head with closed mouth and inset glass eyes. She is on a gusseted kid body with nicely modeled bisque lower arms. In the 1880s (before the invention of the bent-limb baby body), dolls of this type were dressed as babies. *Coleman Collection. Photograph by Thelma Bateman.*

Illustration 104. Alt, Beck & Gottschalck mold 1362, a dolly face with character, which dates after 1910. The expression is quite pert, making this a popular model with collectors. She is 19in (48cm) tall. *Mary Lou Rubright Collection.*

Illustration 105. A pouty closed-mouth doll incised "X" by J.D. Kestner of about 1880. These pouty dolls are very much admired by collectors. The fine quality bisque is delicately tinted. The socket head is on a jointed composition body with straight wrists. She is 15in (38cm) tall. *H&J Foulke, Inc.*

Illustration 106. Here is a lovely 16in (41cm) Kestner with open mouth and two molded upper teeth. She probably dates about 1888. *Sue Bear Collection.*

Illustration 108. A totally original and unplayed-with Kestner doll, she has no mold number, but is marked with the Kestner size "J 13" on the head. Her jointed composition body has the Kestner "Excelsior" stamp. She is 21in (53cm) tall. *H&J Foulke, Inc.*

OPPOSITE PAGE: Illustration 109. Simon & Halbig registered mold 719 in 1887. It is their earliest registered number, although they did make heads before this one — lovely molded hair ladies and some lady shoulder head models with glass eyes and wigs. The face is very appealing with excellent bisque, a fitting doll for competition with the French products. She is 23in (58cm) tall and on a jointed composition body. *Dr. Carole Stoessel Zvonar Collection.*

Illustration 107. This is a cute little 13in (33cm) Kestner 167 mold child with pert and appealing face from about 1900. *H&J Foulke, Inc.*

TOP LEFT: Illustration 110. A 15in (38cm) shoulder head doll by Kling from mold 377 for Kämmer & Reinhardt. She has a very appealing small face and interesting light brown molded eyebrows. She is all original on a cloth body. *H&J Foulke, Inc.*

LEFT: Illustration 111. Simon & Halbig porcelain factory registered mold 908 in 1888. Apparently, not too many of these heads were made as it is a difficult-to-find doll. It has a closed mouth with a white space between the lips; the paperweight eyes have a shaded and threaded iris. The doll has a jointed composition body. She is 17in (43cm) tall. *Richard Wright Collection.*

TOP RIGHT: Illustration 112. A Simon & Halbig doll from mold 939 with open mouth and upper teeth. This mold was registered in 1888 and also came with a closed mouth. The doll is 13in (33cm) tall on a jointed composition body. *H&J Foulke, Inc.* (For a color photograph of this mold number, see page 60.)

Illustration 113. This delightful girl is a Simon & Halbig doll, mold 1039 with flirty eyes. She is an example of the French using a German head, as she is on a Roullet & Decamps clockwork mechanical body, which allows her to walk and move her eyes. *Richard Wright Antiques.*

RIGHT: Illustration 114. This is a beautiful 28in (71cm) example of Simon & Halbig's mold 1249 *Santa*, registered in 1898, which was made for Hamburger & Co., who registered the trademark in 1900. This line was advertised through 1910. *Santa* is characterized by the triangular shading on her lower lip. This mold is very popular with collectors. Since not all 1249 dolls are incised "Santa," S & H apparently also sold this mold to other producers. Mold 1249 always has the same face, whether it is incised "Santa" or not. *H&J Foulke, Inc.*

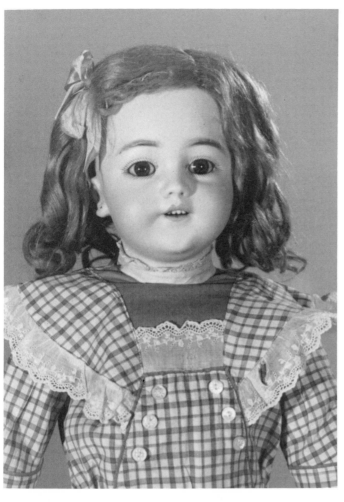

OPPOSITE PAGE: Illustration 115. S & H mold number 600 is a very difficult one to find. It has a more character-type face than some of the other dolly models. This doll is 18in (46cm) tall. *Mary Lou Rubright Collection.*

TOP LEFT: Illustration 116. This is an example of S & H mold 1248, which is really the same as 1249, including the shading on the lower lip. This doll is all original, 24in (61cm) tall. *H&J Foulke, Inc.*

LEFT: Illustration 117. A. Wislizenus of Waltershausen was an old doll factory dating from 1851. They bought heads from Simon & Halbig, Bähr & Pröschild, Ernst Heubach and probably others, as well. Wislizenus is best known for his innovative composition bodies. This dolly face girl marked "A.W. Special" has a sweet heart-shaped face with large glass eyes. *Carter Craft Dollhouse Collection. Photograph by Thelma Bateman.*

TOP RIGHT: Illustration 118. The Gans & Seyfarth doll factory was located in Waltershausen, but was a late entry as it was not established until 1908. This pretty 23in (58cm) doll marked "G & S" has nicely molded eyebrows. *Joanna Ott Collection.*

Illustration 119. This child from the C.M. Bergmann doll factory in Waltershausen, established in 1888, has a head made to Bergmann's order by Simon & Halbig, as the head is incised with the names of both factories. She is 22in (56cm) tall. *Carter Craft Dollhouse Collection. Photograph by Thelma Bateman.*

Illustration 121. This 24in (61cm) girl is incised "Dollar Princess," a line of Kley & Hahn dolls. She has a very sweet face. *Mary Lou Rubright Collection.*

Illustration 120. The Kley & Hahn doll factory was established in 1902 in Ohrdruf. This 30in (76cm) girl is incised "Walkure," a K & H trademark. The head was made by the Kestner factory. *Carter Craft Dollhouse Collection. Photograph by Thelma Bateman.*

Illustration 122. The Max Handwerck doll factory, located in Waltershausen, was established in 1900. Mold 283-28.5 has a delightful, almost smiling face popular with collectors of German dolly-faced dolls who are always looking for an unusual one, but not many Max Handwerck dolls are found. She is 20in (51cm) tall, and totally original in her fancy lace and ribbon-trimmed dress. *H&J Foulke, Inc.*

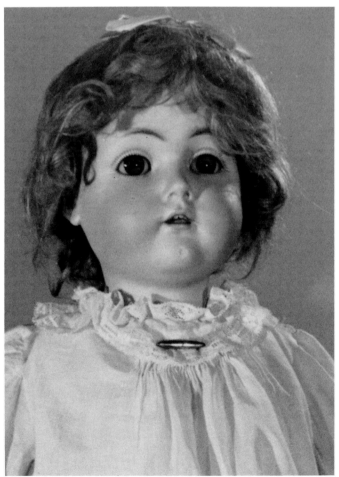

CLOCKWISE: **Illustration 123.** Heinrich Handwerck's doll factory developed into one of the largest and most prosperous in Waltershausen. His dolls were known in the United States for their excellent quality. Simon & Halbig made the heads from Handwerck's own designs. Mold 109 is a favorite with collectors. This 17in (43cm) child is all original in her white cotton dress with lace trim. *H&J Foulke, Inc.*

Illustration 124. Kämmer & Reinhardt of Waltershausen, founded in 1885, was another large doll factory. This doll incised only "192" is an early K & R model (formerly erroneously attributed to Kestner), probably dating from 1892. It is not known which factory made this head for K & R, but it certainly is an Ohrdruf area product. *H&J Foulke, Inc.*

Illustration 125. This 25in (64cm) K & R doll from mold 403 was made for them by Simon & Halbig. She has a very appealing face and is a walking model with turning head which was trademarked by K & R in 1903. The walking doll was still being offered in 1927. *H&J Foulke, Inc.*

Illustration 126. A 24in (61cm) example of mold 109 with large eyes and heavy eyebrows which give her a very French look. Under their *Bebe Cosmopolite* trademark, Heinrich Handwerck supplied heads in the Paris genre to the American market. *H&J Foulke, Inc.*

Sonneberg Area Dolls

TOP LEFT: Illustration 127. By the time bisque dolls became popular, the Dressel family was well established in the doll business having begun distributing toys as far back as 1700. This Dressel shoulder head marked "COD 93," was made for them in 1893 by Armand Marseille, and is one of Marseille's best molds of excellent quality. This 17in (43cm) shoulder head is incised with the wing trademark of Dressel. She is all original. *H&J Foulke, Inc.*

TOP RIGHT: Illustration 128. This 26in (66cm) dolly face incised "C.O.D." is on a jointed composition body. Her face is quite unusual with small eyes and very long cheeks. *Mary Lou Rubright Collection.*

LEFT: Illustration 129. The Recknagle porcelain factory was founded in 1886. This doll is incised with their "R.A." mark. The quality of the heads is uneven, so one must be chosen carefully. *Carter Craft Dollhouse Collection. Photograph by Thelma Bateman.*

Illustration 130. The Gebrüder Kühnlenz porcelain factory opened in 1884. (Previously the dolls marked "G.K." had been erroneously attributed to Gebr. Krauss.) This 23in (58cm) doll is mold 165. *Sheila Needle Collection.*

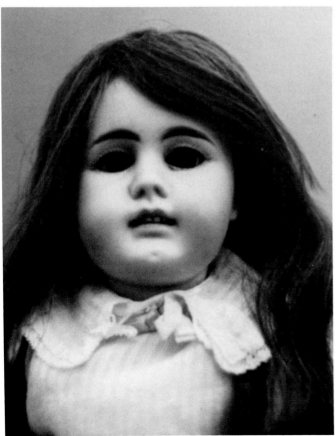

LEFT: Illustration 131. This popular early model by Kühnlenz is incised "41-28" and has almost a character look. Her face is very appealing with small eyes, heavy eyebrows, long cheeks and a distinctive mouth. She is 19in (48cm) tall on an early wood and composition jointed body. *H&J Foulke, Inc.*

RIGHT: Illustration 132. The Schoenau & Hoffmeister porcelain factory was founded in 1901 under the name Porzellanfabrik Burggrub. This 14in (36cm) dolly is from their mold 5800. She is totally original as some little girl received her for Christmas in the early 1900s. *H&J Foulke, Inc.* (For a color photograph of a Schoenau & Hoffmesiter doll, see page 60.)

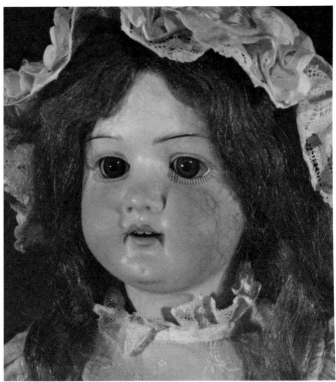

CLOCKWISE: Illustration 133.
The Gebrüder Ohlhaver doll factory opened in 1912, a fairly latecomer to the industry. This doll head incised "150" was made for him by either Gebrüder Heubach or Porzellanfabrik Mengersgereuth. This is a model well-liked by collectors because of the alert expression. The doll was designed to have real upper eyelashes and has painted lower lashes which are long and straight. Sometimes this mold carries the "Revalo" trademark. She is 17in (43cm) tall on a jointed composition body. *H&J Foulke, Inc.*

Illustration 134. The Ernst Heubach porcelain factory was established in 1887. This is their standard dolly face socket head mold 250 which comes on a jointed composition body. She is 24in (61cm) tall. *H&J Foulke, Inc.*

Illustration 135. This chubby-faced little girl with a prominent chin dimple and philtrum is *Mabel*, one of a series of shoulder heads incised with girls names made by Armand Marseille. She has a kid body with bisque lower arms. *M. Elaine Buser.*

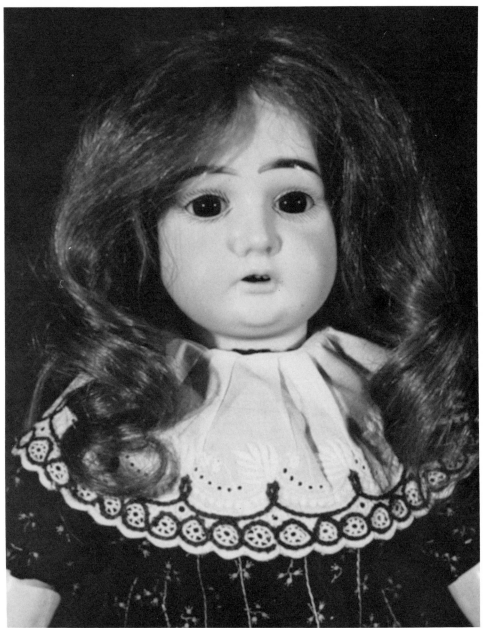

Illustration 136. Armand Marseille, in spite of his French name, was a German manufacturer who owned both a porcelain and doll factory; established in 1884, it was a very large enterprise. This rare mold number 2000 doll was registered in 1895. She is a very desirable A.M. doll with beautiful smooth bisque, a socket head on a ball-jointed composition body, 15in (38cm) tall. *H&J Foulke, Inc.*

OPPOSITE PAGE: Illustration 138. The most beautiful A.M. child doll is the 1894 mold, which is also the year of its inception. Most of these dolls are of excellent quality, and are popular with collectors also because of the sweet face. The socket head models are finer, and are more desirable than the shoulder head models. This close-up view of an A.M. 1894 shows just how appealing the face can be. She is 22in (56cm) tall on a jointed composition body. *H&J Foulke, Inc.*

Illustration 137. *Queen Louise* was made by Armand Marseille for the New York importers, Louis Wolf & Co. She dates from 1910. The pictured *Queen Louise* is 26in (66cm) tall on a jointed composition body. *Carter Craft Dollhouse Collection. Photograph by Thelma Bateman.*

Illustration 139. This 22in (56cm) girl is *My Sweetheart* made for B. Illfelder & Co., a New York and German import-export house. They made this line from 1910 into the 1920s. The doll is incised "B.J. & Co.," but in German I & J may be interchanged. *Mary Lou Rubright Collection.*

Illustration 140. This 24in (61cm) doll is marked on the jointed composition body "Miss Viola" and is perhaps from the *Viola* line of Hamburger & Co., the New York import house. Her head is marked simply "Made in Germany." She is all original. *H&J Foulke, Inc.*

Illustration 141. It is sometimes difficult to determine whether dolls are French or German, and this unmarked Belton-type could be either. She is 19in (48cm) tall. *Richard Wright Antiques.*

Illustration 142. This 14½in (37cm) doll is another unmarked Belton-type of very fine quality, which could be either French or German. *Joyce Alderson Collection.*

C. German Bisque Black, Oriental and Indian Dolls

It appears that most of the German bisque dolls made to represent people other than Caucasians were made after 1888, as they have open mouths. During the 1890s, catalogs offered quite a few models. In 1896, *The Youth's Companion* offered *Happy Family*, a set of five dolls with bisque heads, including an Oriental, a Black and an Indian. These small dolls at 9 or 10in (23 or 25cm) were priced at $1.40 for the set.

Mary Hillier credits Simon & Halbig as being the first German factory to make non-Caucasian dolls, but nearly all doll factories followed suit to produce these dolls, which were particularly popular in England and the United States. It was a time of empire expansion, as well as travel and trading opportunities. The world was opening up and people were becoming curious about people in other lands. Hence, it was a golden opportunity to make dolls to take advantage of this situation.

At first, the black dolls were merely the same as the white ones, simply tinted black. But with the advent of the character dolls in 1909, black dolls with natural features were also designed. (See color photograph on page 60.) These are the most desired by today's doll collectors. They were produced by quite a few companies, including Simon & Halbig, Armand Marseille and Heubach Köppelsdorf. Apparently, black babies were popular in England as quite a few of the bisque ones are found there today.

The bisque head dolls made to represent Orientals are particularly attractive with their creamy gold complexions, dark eyes and black mohair wigs. There is a great demand among collectors for these unique dolls. Simon & Halbig, Armand Marseille, Bähr & Pröschild and J.D. Kestner made the majority of the Oriental dolls, but Schoenau & Hoffmeister made a girl and some have been found unmarked. Ciesliks say that Simon & Halbig applied for a copyright in 1893 for a Chinese child. In 1904, a 13in (33cm) "Geisha Girl" was offered in a wholesale catalog for 50¢ each wholesale, dressed in "fancy silk kimono" and "attractive head dress." Butler Brothers offered Japanese lady dolls with bisque heads, natural glass eyes and exposed teeth at 72¢ each wholesale for a 16in (41cm) doll, dressed in Japanese kimonos with shoes and socks.

LEFT: Illustration 143. This cute 12in (31cm) black child incised only "1000" was made by an unidentified porcelain factory. She is on a jointed composition body. (This mold also has been found in white.) *H&J Foulke, Inc.*

Illustration 144. This Simon & Halbig 1249 doll is seldom found in black bisque. She has thickly molded black glossy eyebrows and thick curly eyelashes. She is 19in (48cm) tall. *Mary Lou Rubright Collection.*

Illustration 145. Judging from the numbers turning up today, very few black dolls were manufactured by Kestner. This is a 12in (31cm) child on a jointed composition body. *H&J Foulke, Inc.*

Illustration 146. Mold number 1358 by Simon & Halbig is a favorite with doll collectors because of its distinct Negroid features. In coloring, it comes from pale chocolate to charcoal black. Her nose is broad with flared nostrils and her lips are very full. Her opened mouth shows six upper teeth. Her molded eyebrows are painted glossy black. She is 18in (46cm) tall. *Mary Lou Rubright Collection.*

OPPOSITE PAGE: Illustration 149. The Schützmeister & Quendt porcelain factory made this realistic character baby head, mold 251. It has very wide red lips and a curly black mohair wig. She is 21in (53cm) tall on a bent-limb baby body. *India Stoessel Collection.*

Illustration 147. Simon & Halbig made mold 101 for Kämmer & Reinhardt in 1909. It was one of the first K & R bisque character dolls. Very rarely is a brown bisque model found. This one is 12in (31cm) tall. *Richard Wright Collection.*

Illustration 148. Even though the A.M. 351 is probably the most commonly found black bisque baby, it is still very popular as it is very appealing, more so in black than in the ubiquitous white model. This one is 14in (36cm) tall on a composition bent-limb baby body. *H&J Foulke, Inc.*

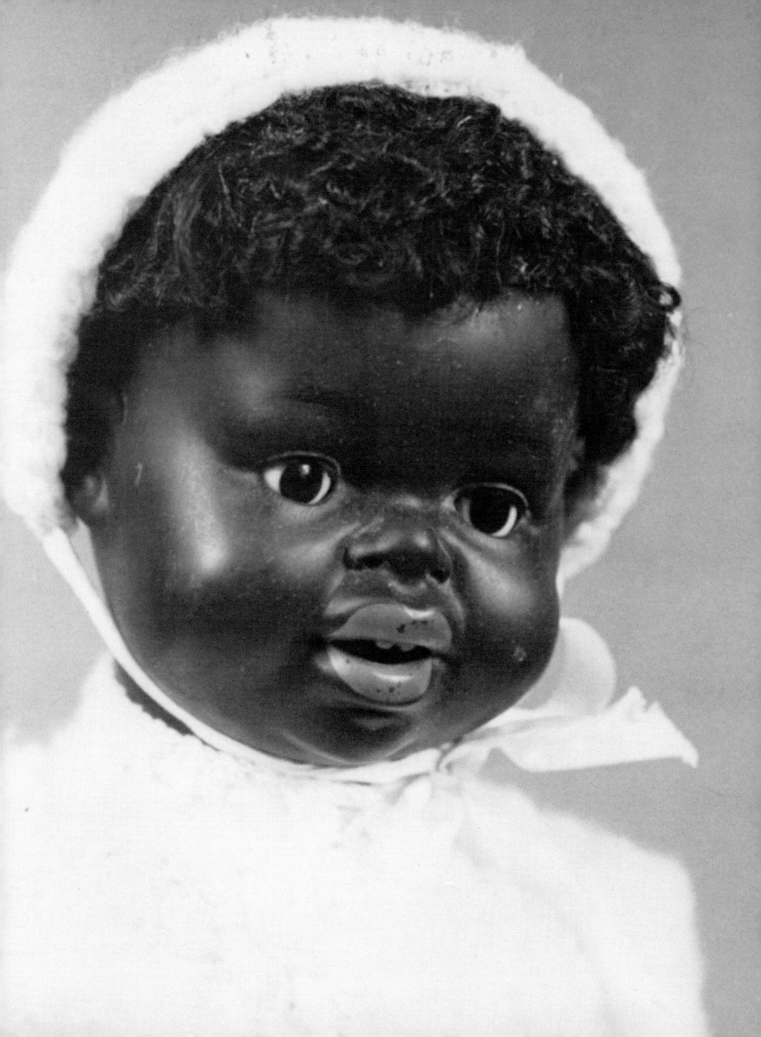

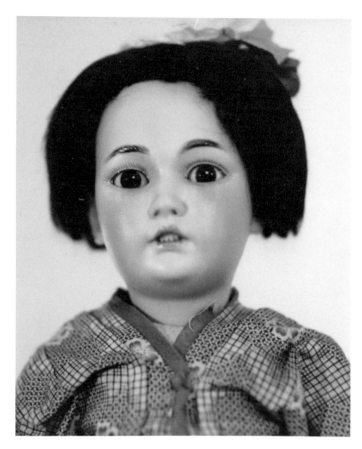

TOP LEFT: Illustration 150. This very rare Oriental doll was made by Bähr & Pröschild for Bruno Schmidt and incised with "B.S.W." in a heart. She has a lovely complexion, slanted black multi-stroked eyebrows, almond-shaped black eyes and pierced ears. She is 19in (48cm) tall on a ball-jointed composition body. *Richard Wright Antiques.*

TOP RIGHT: Illustration 151. This is mold 1329 by Simon & Halbig with a lovely creamy gold complexion and molded black eyebrows. She is 16in (41cm) tall on a jointed composition body. *H&J Foulke, Inc.*

LEFT: Illustration 152. The most popular and most expensive German Oriental doll is this baby, mold 243, by J.D. Kestner. It is a socket head on a bent-limb baby body. It is an incredible doll with chubby cheeks, tiny dark eyes with upper painted lashes, wispy dark eyebrows and black mohair wig. The pictured doll is 14in (36cm) tall and all original. *Richard Wright Collection.*

OPPOSITE PAGE: Illustration 153. This Oriental doll with closed mouth was made by Bähr & Pröschild about 1888. She is one of the few Orientals found with a closed mouth. She has a socket head on a jointed composition body, 15in (38cm) tall. *Mary Lou Rubright Collection.*

Illustration 154. Here are two Oriental dolls: a 6in (15cm) A.M. 351 (usually found in white) and a 9in (23cm) A.M. 353 Oriental baby (used only for Orientals). Both are on tinted cream composition bent-limb baby bodies. *Jimmy & Faye Rodolfos Collection.*

BELOW: Illustration 156. Dolls to represent American Indians were made by Armand Marseille with fairly ordinary appearance, but it took Gebrüder Heubach with their marvelous character interpretations to sculpt this Indian doll, mold number 8457. This is a shoulder head doll with cloth body and composition arms and legs. She has a gray mohair wig with braid. *Richard Wright Collection.*

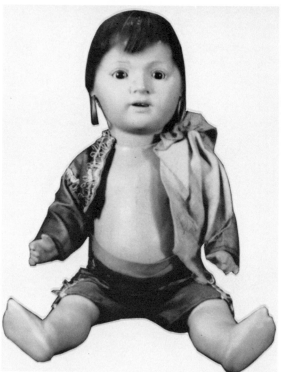

Illustration 155. Ernst Heubach of Köppelsdorf made several molds to represent non-Caucasians. This is number 452, with molded hair and pierced ears, which usually appears in a reddish color. He is 12in (31cm) tall on a five-piece composition toddler body. *Richard Wright Antiques.*

D. German Bisque Character Children

By the turn of the century (1900), there were many people who were beginning to be disenchanted by this gorgeous creature, the French or French-type doll. Rumblings were heard in German society about the unnaturalness of the French doll and her lack of reality. This was a time of great social change with a developing interest in psychology, as well. It was a time of emerging importance of the human being, and emphasis on the individual. There was a general turn from ostentation to simplicity, a taste for the photographic and literal. All of these things helped bring about the Munich Movement of the early 1900s. The social climate was right for a change, and artists began working on new doll designs. They were attempting to depart from the stereotypical doll face and turn toward naturalism, a face with a realistic expression and child-like features. Their goal was to create a doll that looked real, one modeled from a living child. Käthe Kruse was one of the first to achieve success in this line. Marion Kaulitz with her *Munich Art Dolls* was credited as being the moving force behind this essentially German doll reform movement.

There is no doubt that Kämmer & Reinhardt were in the forefront of the character doll movement, and it is in this area of doll making that the company made its greatest contribution. With the development of this new realistic style in 1909, the Germans had a design uniquely their own. In their Anniversary Booklet of 1911, K & R recognized that the criticism of the old-style German doll was justified. They, themselves, had been using virtually the same model for 23 years. Although they thought the new models presented at the Munich Exposition were ugly, except in regard to regional costumes, they did see merit in this new idea. Therefore, they consulted a well-known artist in Berlin. When he showed them a bronze bust of a six-week-old baby, they recognized the beauty of the head, but were hesitant to produce it as a doll because it was so realistic. Yet, they followed their hunches, and the result was the famous "Baby," mold 100. (See *Illustration 187*.) The heads for the bisque K & R character dolls were poured for them by Simon & Halbig from K & R's own designs. In April 1909, Strobel & Wilken Co. ran the first of their ads in *Playthings* for character dolls by K & R, which were advertised as "produced from life models." Eventually, the character dolls became quite successful, with every porcelain factory following K & R's lead to produce character dolls. Even so, the dolly face model continued to dominate the doll market, and the character doll never did surpass her in quantity produced.

Unfortunately, the character child movement was fairly short lived; hence, the character children are difficult, some models nearly impossible, to find today. Within a few years, the character babies were taking over the market. They are charming and cute and sweet, but they lack the artistry and presence of the character child, the German doll makers' crowning achievement.

Waltershausen/ Ohrdruf Area

Illustration 157. Kämmer & Reinhardt's first character models from 1909 included mold 101, which was available as a girl, *Marie*, or as a boy, *Peter*. This lovely example of *Marie* is 20in (51cm) tall on a jointed toddler body. *Richard Wright Collection.*

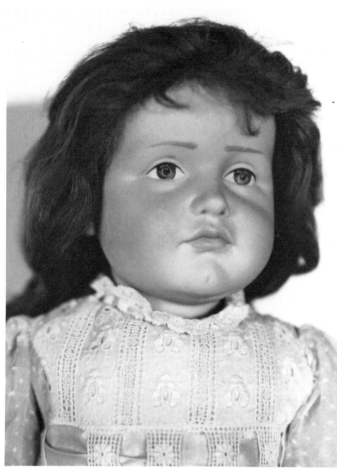

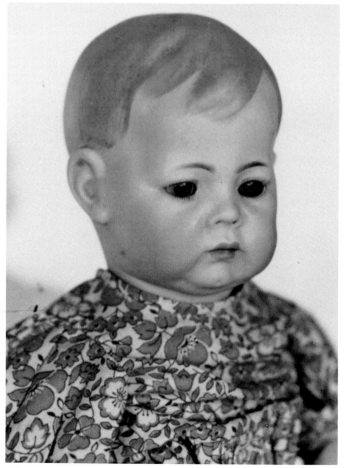

TOP LEFT: Illustration 158. Kämmer & Reinhardt character child *Elise*, mold number 109. This very pensive-faced child is not commonly found. She is 22in (56cm) tall on a jointed composition body. *Richard Wright Antiques.*

TOP RIGHT: Illustration 159. A very favorite K & R character with collectors is mold number 114: *Gretchen* as a girl and *Hans* as a boy. This lovely pouty *Gretchen* has rarely found brown eyes. She has wonderfully sharp modeling and is 24in (61cm) tall. *Richard Wright Collection.*

LEFT: Illustration 160. K & R model 115 registered in 1911 is the first of the character children to have glass eyes. During the early years of production K & R could not solve the problem of inserting the sleeping eyes. Apparently, it was difficult to put sleeping eyes into the heads without disadvantaging the facial expression. This pouty-type model with molded hair was apparently very popular as several porcelain factories made similar dolls; the same style appeared in cloth (Kruse), wood (Schoenhut) and celluloid (Bruno Schmidt). *Richard Wright Collection.*

RIGHT: Illustration 161. K & R mold 116 molded hair is fairly difficult to find, 116A with a wig turns up more often. This 20in (51cm) doll is on a baby body, although the model comes also as a toddler. *Richard Wright Collection.*

BOTTOM LEFT: Illustration 162. K & R mold 117 or 117A with a closed mouth, both with the same face, are very sought-after models. The model was registered in 1911. The pouty-style face is particularly appealing and collectors like the feature of sleeping eyes, missing on most of the earlier child models. Here is a 22in (56cm) example of K & R mold 117, with the same face as 117A. *H&J Foulke, Inc.*

BOTTOM RIGHT: Illustration 163. This 24in (61cm) example of K & R 117n has the usual open mouth with four upper curved teeth. Some of this model, which was registered in 1916, have flirty eyes. This model was made until the 1930s. *H&J Foulke, Inc.* (For other K & R characters, see color photographs on page 62.)

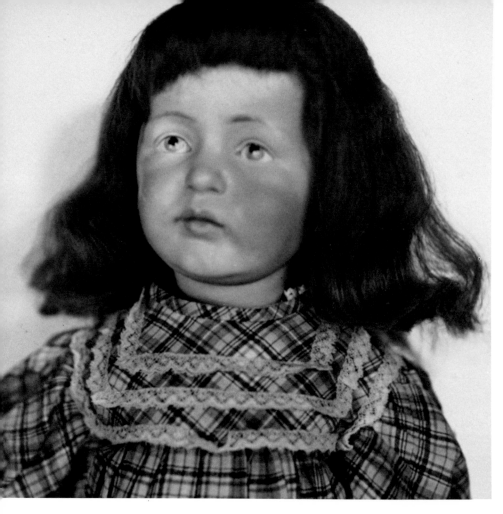

OPPOSITE PAGE: **Illustration 166.**
Simon & Halbig made the character dolls for K & R, but also a line of their own designs and models for other companies, as well. Although this model, mold 120, carries only the S & H initials, Ciesliks say the head was made for K & R. She is 20in (51cm) tall. *Mary Lou Rubright Collection.*

Illustration 164. The Kestner factory did not produce many character children. This is one of their rarest models, mold 208, in a very large 24in (61cm) size. She has wonderful, realistic modeling. *Richard Wright Collection.*

Illustration 165. This J.D.K. mold 221 googly is certainly one of the most mischievous and flirtatious of character dolls. She has a socket head on a jointed composition toddler body. This model is 13in (33cm) tall. *Richard Wright Collection.* (For a color photograph of this mold, see page 62.)

TOP LEFT: Illustration 167. This Simon & Halbig child is mold 1279. As she dates from 1899, she is not really a character child, yet she does have a very distinctive face with slanted eyebrows, dimples and a triangle of shading in the center of her lower lip. Collectors pay a character doll price for her. This lovely doll is 28in (71cm) tall. *Richard Wright Collection.*

TOP RIGHT: Illustration 168. Bähr & Pröschild made some beautiful character dolls for Bruno Schmidt. The B & P factory was well known for its high quality bisque. One of the most sought-after Bruno Schmidt dolls is mold 2033, referred to by American collectors as *Wendy*. She has a closed pouty mouth with fairly wide lips and glass sleeping eyes. This example is 18in (46cm) tall. *Private Collection.*

LEFT: Illustration 169. Another beautiful Bähr & Pröschild doll, mold 546 for Kley & Hahn. She is a rarely found model. The doll is 21in (53cm) tall. *Richard Wright Collection.* (For another Bähr & Pröschild/Kley & Hahn character doll, see color photograph on page 63.)

CLOCKWISE: Illustration 170. Hertel, Schwab & Co. are responsible for a group of exceptional googly dolls. Although a late arrival on the doll scene in 1910, this Ohrdruf porcelain factory did exceptionally good work. Until recently, their dolls were attributed to J.D. Kestner and, indeed, the factories were in the same town. This example of mold 163 looks somewhat like a *Campbell Kid* with reddish molded hair, glass eyes looking to the side, and open/closed watermelon mouth with protruding upper lip. She is 17in (43cm) tall. *Richard Wright Antiques.*

Illustration 171. This Hertel, Schwab & Co. googly is mold 173. He has a whimsical watermelon mouth with painted lips. He is 16in (41cm) tall on a toddler body. *Richard Wright Collection.*

Illustration 172. One of the most beautiful Hertel, Schwab & Co. character dolls is mold 134. She has wavy stroked eyebrows typical of Hertel, Schwab & Co. Her closed mouth has sensuous lips. She is 15in (38cm) tall. *Mary Lou Rubright Collection.*

Lichte Area

Illustration 174. One of the favorite Gebrüder Heubach dolls with open mouth is mold 8192, probably a model designed to compete with other manufacturers' dolly face dolls. However, this Heubach girl has a lot more personality than an ordinary dolly face model. She is a socket head on a jointed composition body. *H&J Foulke, Inc.*

Illustration 173. Although the Gebrüder Heubach porcelain factory was established in 1804, it was not until 1910 that this factory began to make bisque doll heads. This tiny 8½in (22cm) toddler appears to be mold 5636 with open/closed mouth and lower molded teeth, their first model. *Richard Wright Antiques.*

Illustration 175. The Gebrüder Heubach pouty dolls with glass eyes are very sought-after by collectors. This pouty Heubach girl, 16in (41cm) tall with closed mouth and tiny glass eyes, is on a jointed composition body. *Richard Wright Antiques.*

Sonneberg Area

Illustration 176. "Revalo" dolls were produced by Gebrüder Ohlhaver of Sonneberg from 1912 on from heads made by Gebrüder Heubach, Ernst Heubach and Porzellanfabrik Mengersgereuth and are of surprisingly good quality for Sonneberg heads. This pair of 12in (31cm) tall character dolls marked "Revalo" both have molded hair and painted eyes. *Mary Goolsby.*

BELOW: Illustration 177. The Goebel porcelain factory, although established earlier, started making dolls in 1887. Their most interesting dolls are the series of small character girls with various hair styles, most decorated with flowers and ribbons. This cute girl with open/closed smiling mouth and molded teeth, is just 6½in (17cm) tall. *H&J Foulke, Inc.*

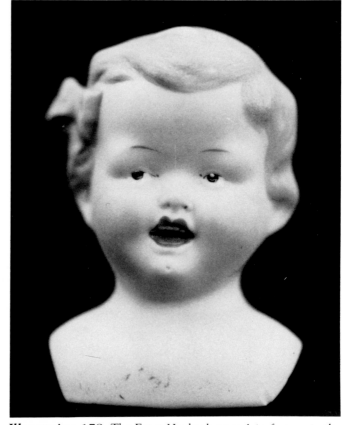

Illustration 178. The Ernst Heubach porcelain factory in the Köppelsdorf/Sonneberg area is better known for dolly faces and character babies than children. But the factory did produce a series of shoulder head characters with molded hair and painted eyes as well as a series of small googly-eyed dolls. This bisque head is mold 262. *H&J Foulke, Inc.*

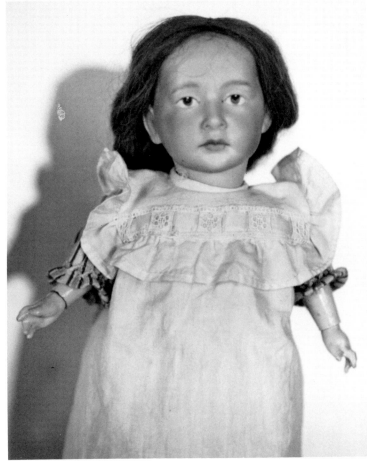

TOP LEFT: Illustration 179. As far as is known to date, this is the only model character child which has been found with the C.O.D. mark of Cuno & Otto Dressel of Sonneberg, a very old doll factory. Apparently, this was their own design poured for them by an unidentified porcelain factory. She is 17in (43cm) tall on a jointed composition body. *Esther Schwartz Collection.*

TOP RIGHT: Illustration 180. Armand Marseille, judging from the numbers of dolls found today, must have had the largest porcelain and doll factory in Sonneberg. This 16in (41cm) character girl is a very rare model, having intaglio eyes and wide pouty lips. She is on a jointed composition body. *Richard Wright Collection.*

LEFT: Illustration 181. One of the sweetest A.M. character children is mold 550, slightly smiling with dimples and tiny sleeping eyes. She is a socket head on a jointed composition body. *Richard Wright Collection.*

Illustration 182. This 10in (25cm) A.M. 250 character boy, registered in 1912, was made for George Borgfeldt and used on a jointed composition body. It is not an easily found doll. *Betty Harms Collection.*

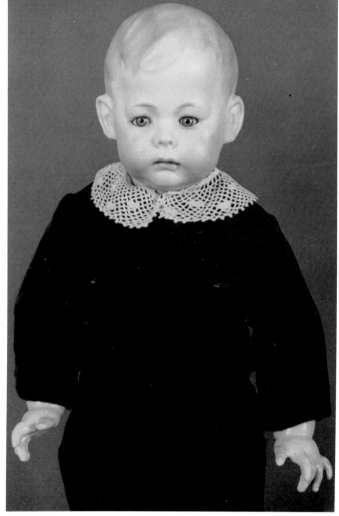

Illustration 183. The most pricey and desirable of the A.M. character children is *Fany*, mold 230 with molded hair or mold 231 with wig. *Fany* was registered in 1912 and made by A.M. for George Borgfeldt. Molds 230 and 231 both come on desirable jointed composition toddler bodies. This outstanding example of mold 230 with molded hair is 19in (48cm) tall. *Richard Wright Collection.*

101

Illustration 184. This A.M. 253 googly is favored over all the other A.M. googlies. She is just so impish; she brings a smile to everyone's lips. Particularly desirable on the 253 model are the sleeping glass eyes and the watermelon-slice-shaped mouth. This particular doll is 10in (25cm), a larger size than usually found. *H&J Foulke, Inc.*

Illustration 185. A.M. 310 *Just Me* is a delightful little girl with side-glancing and sleeping eyes and tiny mouth. She is a fairly late doll from the 1920s and 1930s and comes on a five-piece composition child body. She came in both tinted and sprayed or painted bisque. The tinted bisque model fetches a higher price as the color on the sprayed one tends to peel off as it is not fired a second time to permanently set the color. The pictured 9½in (24cm) *Just Me* is wearing an original tagged Vogue Doll Co. outfit. *H&J Foulke, Inc.*

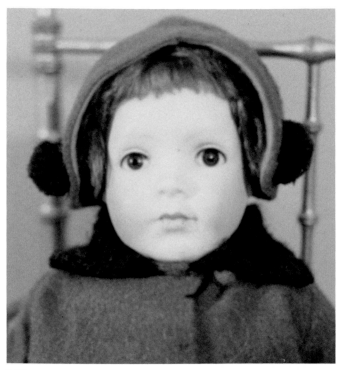

LEFT: Illustration 186. Although Grace Cory Rockwell was an American designer, her bisque head character children had heads made in Germany following the Rockwell designs. Two models are known, a molded hair girl and a wigged one. This wigged girl is 20in (51cm) tall, a shoulder head on a cloth and composition body. Neither of the Rockwell models are found very often. The porcelain factory responsible for making these heads has not been identified. *Private Collection.*

E. German Bisque Character Babies

The character baby era lasted quite a bit longer than the character child one. Judging from their rarity, the character children were made only a few years in comparison to the character babies which were still being manufactured in large quantities until about 1930. Although the smiling character babies are winsome, cuddly and cute, it is unfortunate for collectors today that the creative and innovative designs displayed in the character children were eventually entirely replaced by the smiling character babies. Apparently, the character baby is the doll which ultimately came out the winner from the Munich Art Movement to create a lifelike doll. The numbers of these character babies available today indicates their original popularity. They were made by all of the porcelain factories.

Waltershausen/Ohrdruf Area Dolls

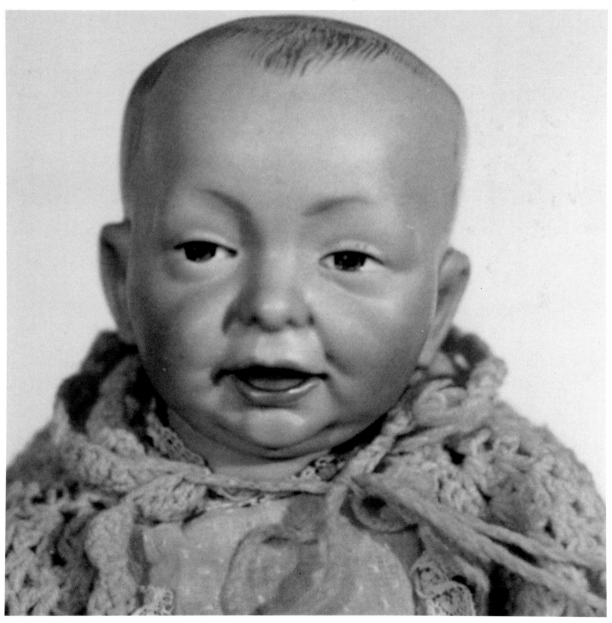

Illustration 187. Here is the famous Kämmer & Reinhardt mold 100 *Baby* which started the character doll movement in bisque. It was modeled by a Berlin artist from a six-week-old baby with lovely natural detail, particularly around the eyes and mouth, even the double chin. Obviously, this was quite a departure from the traditional dolly face. The solid dome head has just a hint of molded hair at the very top of his head and the nape of his neck. His ears are very large with natural looking outer and inner folds. The K & R character heads were made by the Simon & Halbig porcelain factory. *H&J Foulke, Inc.*

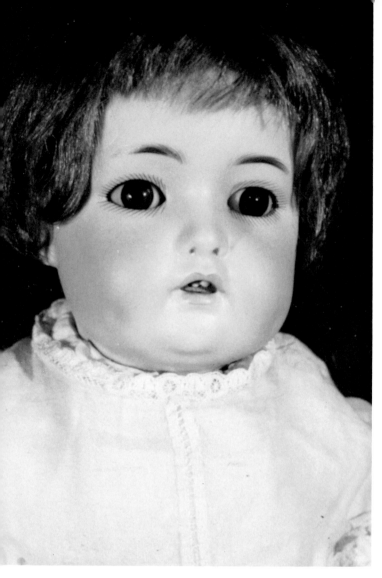

Illustration 188. K & R mold 118A is very difficult to find and is distinguished by three dimples: one in her chin and one placed low on each cheek. She is 14in (36cm) tall. *H&J Foulke, Inc.*

OPPOSITE PAGE: Illustration 190. K & R mold 128 dates from 1914, but is a fairly difficult mold to find in bisque, although the celluloid version 728 was used extensively. It has a very appealing face; the open mouth has two upper teeth and a separate tongue. This cute toddler is 25in (64cm) tall. *Mary Lou Rubright Collection.* (For a color photograph of this mold number, see page 64.)

Illustration 189. K & R mold 126 apparently was a favorite as it continued in production from 1914 until the 1930s. It came with sleeping eyes, flirting eyes or naughty eyes and sometimes with a moving tongue. It was available on a bent-limb baby body, a jointed or unjointed toddler body, and a regular ball-jointed body for some of the larger dolls. It was available with dark as well as white skin. K & R advertised her as "The best and prettiest baby in the world, copied by all, equalled by none." *Coleman Collection. Photograph by Thelma Bateman.*

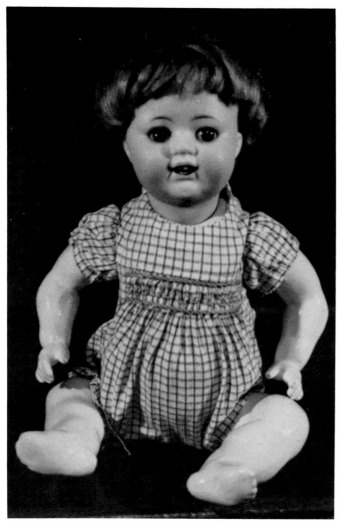

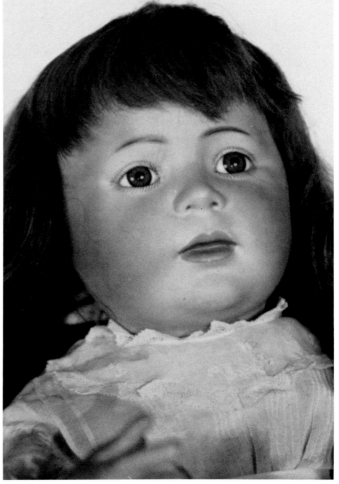

CLOCKWISE: Illustration 191. Although C. M. Bergmann of Waltershausen advertised character babies, very few are found with his name on them. This 12in (31cm) smiling character baby is fully signed "C.M. Bergmann." Many Bergmann dolls were made by Simon & Halbig. *H&J Foulke, Inc.*

Illustration 192. Adolph Hülss began his factory in about 1915 and advertised "highest quality bent-limb babies and toddlers, dressed and undressed." This is Simon & Halbig's mold 156, made especially for Hülss as it also carried his trademark. This toddler in original Tyrolean costume is 9¾in (25cm) tall. *H&J Foulke, Inc.*

Illustration 193. Simon & Halbig character baby mold 1488 also comes on a toddler or jointed body. She has such a pleading expression, as though she wants to be picked up and held. This mold is fairly difficult to find. The pictured baby is 24in (61cm) tall. *Richard Wright Collection.*

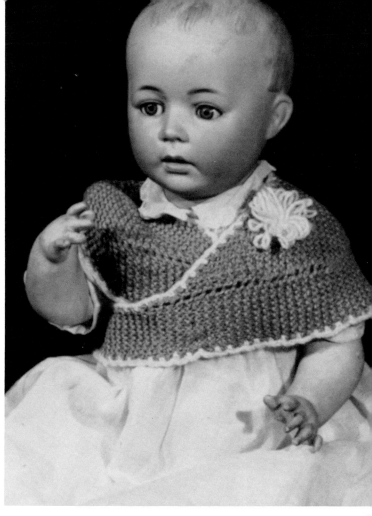

CLOCKWISE: Illustration 194. This rare baby is mold 1498 and appears to be a molded hair version of 1488. He is 19in (48cm) tall. *Richard Wright Antiques.*

Illustration 195. Franz Schmidt opened his doll factory near Waltershausen in 1890. He was a very enterprising gentleman and bisque head dolls were only a part of his line. He claims to have been the first to successfully manufacture character dolls with glass sleeping eyes. Simon & Halbig poured some of the Franz Schmidt heads after his own designs. This large 24in (61cm) character baby is from mold 1295 made by S & H. *H&J Foulke, Inc.*

Illustration 196. This is another Franz Schmidt baby, this one from mold 1271. The porcelain factory which made the head has not been identified, but it is probably a Waltershausen/Ohrdruf area factory. The head has excellent modeling with an open/closed mouth and molded teeth, with much detail around the cheeks and chin. The baby is 12in (31cm) tall. *H&J Foulke, Inc.*

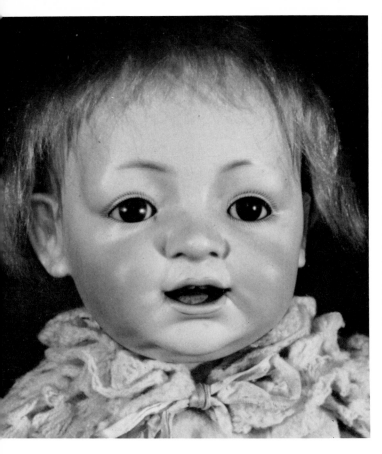

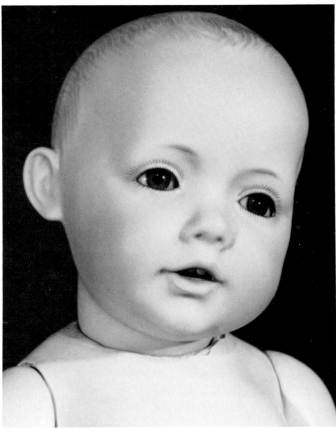

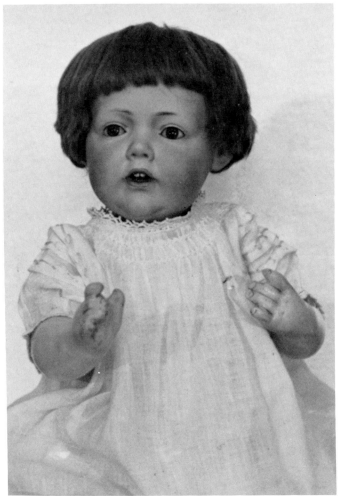

TOP LEFT: Illustration 197. The J.D. Kestner firm made a series of lovely character babies. Kestner owned both a porcelain and doll factory so he could make complete dolls. Mold 226 is really a happy baby. His eyes are large and his mouth is wide open with two upper teeth and a separate tongue. He is on a Kestner bent-limb composition baby body of excellent quality. Kestner bodies always have the left arm and hand curved in. He is 18in (46cm) tall. *H&J Foulke, Inc.*

TOP RIGHT: Illustration 198. The J.D.K. *Hilda* with molded hair is shown in a 1914 Kestner advertisement; some *Hildas* carry the 1914 date incised on the back of their heads. The molded hair model is more difficult to find than the wigged version. She carries the registration number of 1070, but not a mold number. This doll is 16in (41cm) tall. *H&J Foulke, Inc.*

LEFT: Illustration 199. This J.D.K. *Hilda* is from mold 237 and is 14in (36cm) tall. *Hilda* is most favored of all the J.D.K. character babies with collectors and brings astonishing prices. Another *Hilda* mold number is 245. *Rosemary Dent Collection.*

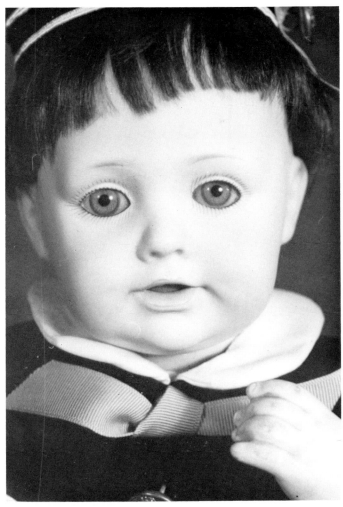

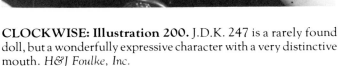

CLOCKWISE: Illustration 200. J.D.K. 247 is a rarely found doll, but a wonderfully expressive character with a very distinctive mouth. *H&J Foulke, Inc.*

Illustration 201. J.D.K. 257 is found frequently and appears to be one of the last character dolls made by the Kestner factory until the 1930s. The sizing on the head is indicated in centimeters instead of the usual Kestner alphabet system. This head is most often found on Kestner bent-limb baby bodies. This 13in (33cm) baby has a curly lamb's wool wig. *H&J Foulke, Inc.*

Illustration 202. This 24in (61cm) J.D.K. 260 toddler is all original and still resides in her original box with blue cloth-covered packing and dust ruffle which was arranged as a bed. Her blue wool dress was made just for her and is trimmed with decorative stitching. Her blue stockings are held up by blue ribbons threaded through the tops. Her body is the most desirable type for a character doll — a jointed toddler one with chubby legs and slant hip joints. *H&J Foulke, Inc.*

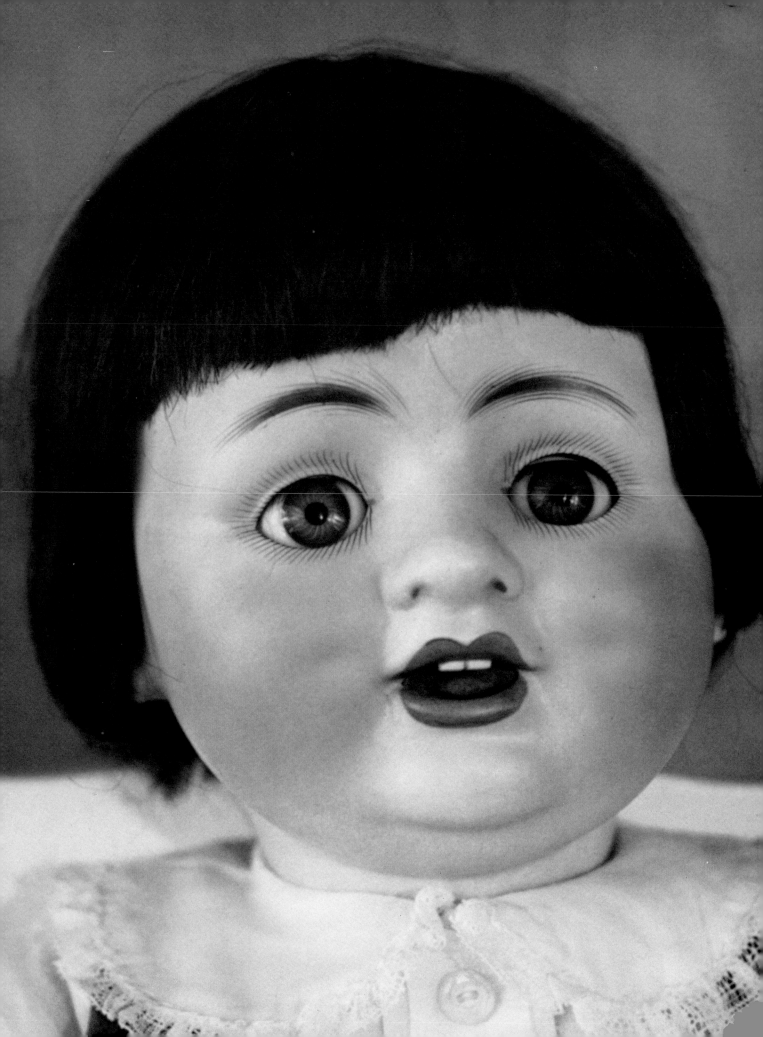

OPPOSITE PAGE: **Illustration 203.** This 22in (56cm) character baby from mold 208 by Catterfelder Puppenfabrik was possibly made for them by J. D. Kestner. It has the centimeter size of 55 on it; the centimeter sizing was used also on the late Kestner character babies. Kestner is known to have made other heads for C.P. *Mary Lou Rubright Collection.*

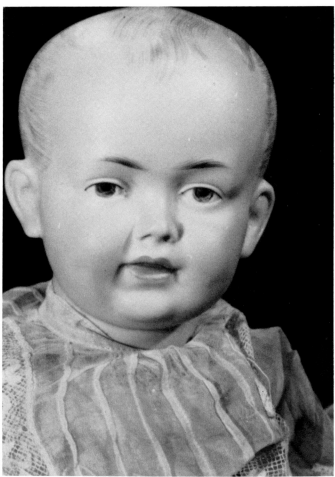

CLOCKWISE: Illustration 204. A 21in (53cm) Kley & Hahn character baby from mold 167. The heads of the Kley & Hahn 100 series dolls were made for them by Hertel, Schwab & Co. They are often distinguished by the so-called "flyaway" eyebrows painted with short slanted wispy strokes. *H&J Foulke, Inc.*

Illustration 205. This character baby head incised only "531" was made for Kley & Hahn by the Bähr & Pröschild porcelain factory. He has deeply molded eye sockets and painted eyes. *H&J Foulke, Inc.*

Illustration 206. A Bähr & Pröschild 624 character baby has a very cute face with cheek dimples. The dolls from the B.P. porcelain factory have excellent quality bisque, and are generally unappreciated by collectors. This baby is 20in (51cm) tall. *Rosemary Dent Collection.*

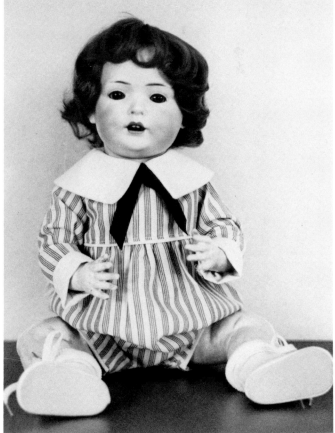

LEFT: Illustration 207. Some Bähr & Pröschild dolls were made for Bruno Schmidt and carry the trademarks of both companies. Bruno Schmidt took over the B.P. factory in 1918. This baby has the BSW initials inside a heart. She is 24in (61cm) tall. *Sheila Needle.*

BOTTOM LEFT: Illustration 208. Alt, Beck & Gottschalck porcelain factory made the head on this character from mold 1352. Beside a well-done character baby face, she has two other desirable features: flirty eyes and a jointed toddler body. *H&J Foulke, Inc.*

BOTTOM RIGHT: Illustration 209. Alt, Beck & Gottschalck made the heads for *Baby Bo Kaye* with the 1394 mold number. This J. L. Kallus designed doll was produced by the Cameo Doll Co. in 1925 and distributed by George Borgfeldt. The pictured 20in (51cm) *Baby Bo Kaye* is all original. *Richard Wright Collection.*

OPPOSITE PAGE: Illustration 210. Alt, Beck & Gottschalck made *Bonnie Babe* designed by Georgene Averill for K & K Toy Co. and George Borgfeldt in 1926. Mold numbers are 1368 and 1402. *Mary Lou Rubright Collection.*

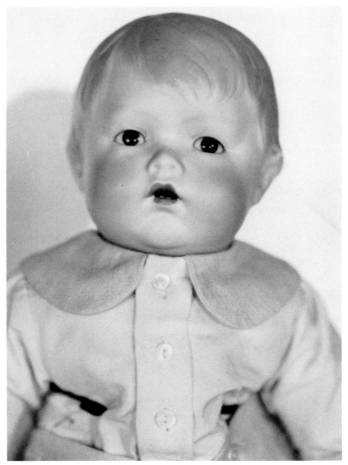

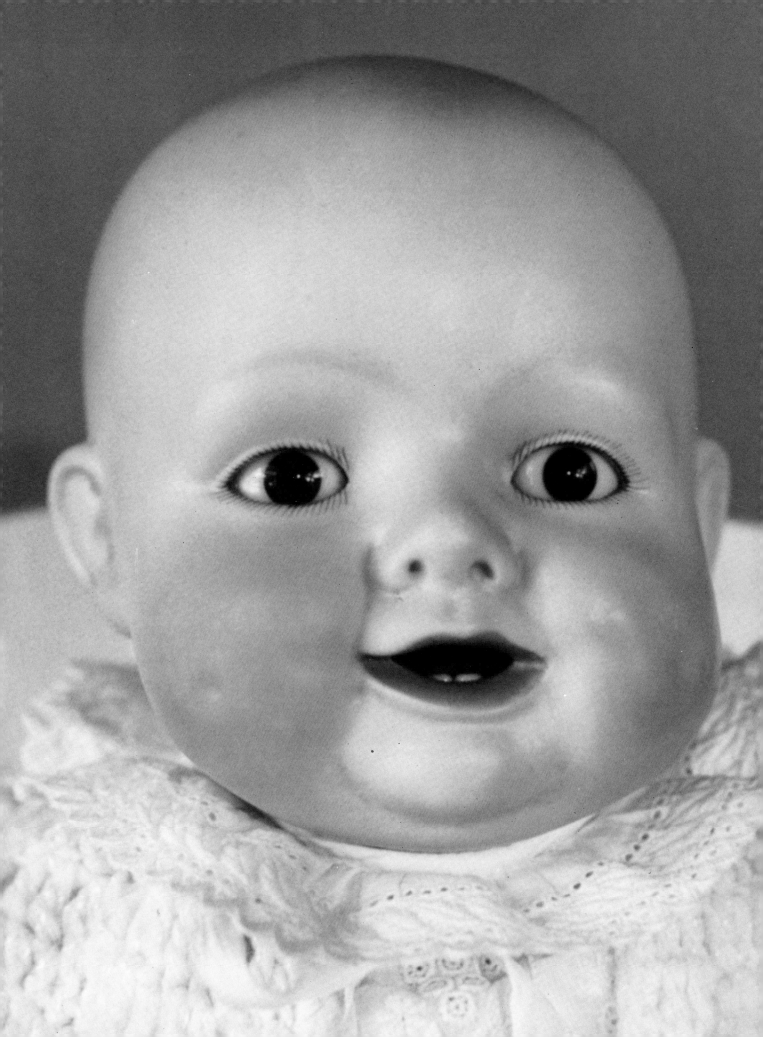

Sonneberg Area Dolls

Illustration 213. An unusual Swaine & Co. mold is on this toddler incised "FO" with the green S & Co. trademark stamp. He has a five-piece composition body and wears original Tyrolean costume. He has intaglio eyes, an open/closed mouth and molded hair. *Richard Wright Antiques.*

(For other S & Co. character dolls, see color photographs on pages 63 and 64.)

TOP LEFT: Illustration 211. Swaine & Co. founded a porcelain factory in 1810, but was not recorded as making dolls until 1910, when they participated in the Leipzig fair with character dolls. This 22in (56cm) baby with open mouth is incised only "232," but other versions carry the name *Lori,* as well. Dolls usually are stamped in green with the S & Co. trademark. *Clendenien Collection.*

LEFT: Illustration 212. Armand Marseille had a very large porcelain factory and made heads for quite a few doll producers as well as his own factory. The A.M. porcelain factory made this character baby with registration number 248 and mold number 251 for George Borgfeldt. It is a favorite face with broad one-stroke eyebrows, tiny sleep eyes with painted lashes, and open/closed mouth with molded tongue between the lips. Mold 251 also comes in an open mouth version which is not quite as cute. *H&J Foulke, Inc.*

OPPOSITE PAGE: Illustration 214. The most famous Swaine & Co. doll is *Lori.* She is incised only with her name, no mold number, but has the green S & Co. stamp. She has an open/closed mouth with very nice molding around her mouth, nose and eyes. Her eyebrows are painted with many tiny strokes and her glass sleeping eyes are rather small. She has a hint of molded hair, just about what one would expect a baby to have. She is 22in (56cm) tall. *Richard Wright Collection.*

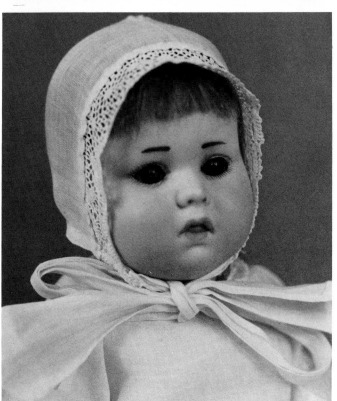

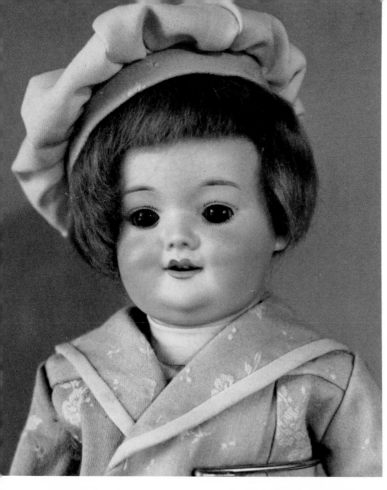

LEFT: Illustration 215. A.M. mold 560a is a cute smiling character face with dimples and very winsome expression. It is usually found on a baby body, sometimes a toddler body. The doll pictured is 15in (38cm) tall. *Mary Lou Rubright Collection.*

BOTTOM LEFT: Illustration 216. This head with A.M. mold number 990 has exceptionally beautiful and smooth bisque. The complexion coat is even and the eyebrows are painted in many individual strokes. Although some of their heads are beautiful, the Marseille factory made many heads which are not as fine a quality as this one. This baby is 17in (43cm) tall. *H&J Foulke, Inc.*

BELOW: Illustration 217. K & K Toy Co. of New York City had bisque shoulder heads made in Germany for use on their mama dolls. It is not known which porcelain factory made these heads. This character boy with open mouth and sleeping eyes is 22in (56cm) tall. The numbers of the backs of the K & K heads probably represent the size in centimeters the doll would have been if the head had been placed on a child size rather than mama doll body, the latter being shorter and chubbier. *H&J Foulke, Inc.*

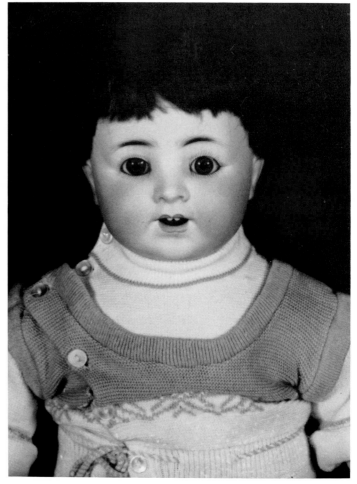

116

Illustration 218. Arthur Schoenau was one of the few Sonneberg doll makers to own both a doll and porcelain factory. The porcelain factory was founded in 1901 with Carl Hoffmeister. The Porzellanfabrik Burggrub was located in the Sonneberg area and supplied heads to many doll factories, including Dressel and Maar & Sohn. Mold 169 was their standard character baby. This example is 24in (61cm) tall. Many collectors confuse this factory with Simon & Halbig as the Schoenau Hoffmeister factory used the S.H. initials, also, but with a star enclosing the initials "PB" for Porzellanfabrik Burggrub. *H&J Foulke, Inc.*

RIGHT: Illustration 219. A favorite Schoenau Hoffmeister character is *Hanna* which comes as a baby or a toddler. She has a very sweet appealing face with wispy stroked eyebrows, real upper eyelashes and straight painted lower ones. Her open mouth has upper teeth. This little toddler is 13in (33cm) tall. *Joanna Ott Collection.*

TOP LEFT: Illustration 220. Porzellanfabrik Burggrub made the bisque heads for the *Princess Elizabeth* dolls beginning in 1929 when she was three years old. The demand was higher than the number of dolls they could make. This example is 21in (53cm). *Richard Wright Antiques.*

TOP RIGHT: Illustration 221. The Ernst Heubach porcelain factory in Köppelsdorf (Sonneberg area) made quite a few very cute laughing character babies. They made heads for companies using the trademarks "Jutta, Igodi, Revalo" and "SUR." as well as others. This large 23in (58cm) Ernst Heubach character baby is from mold 342. *H&J Foulke, Inc.*

LEFT: Illustration 222. The P.M. initials used on this doll represent Porzellanfabrik Mengersgereuth; it is mold 914, one of their standard character babies. He is 22in (56cm) tall. *H&J Foulke, Inc.*

F. German Bisque Infant Dolls

The infant doll was essentially an American development after 1914. However, some of the Sonneberg papier-mâché dolls and some of the English poured wax dolls represented infants as did the china *Frozen Charlottes, London Rag Babies,* and the Nursing Bru. China head dolls were sometimes dressed as ladies, children or babies. Although some bisque head dolls of the 1880s and 1890s were dressed as infants, for example, some of the closed-mouth turned shoulder head dolls and some of the Kestner 143 mold dolls, these dolls were not actually designed as infants. For the most part until 1914, bisque head dolls dressed in infant clothing were the same as those dressed as children.

The first infant doll with a bisque head appears to have been Louis Amberg's *New Born Babe,* copyrighted in 1914. Apparently, it was not an overwhelming success. It was an idea whose time was not yet ready. It was about ten years later that Grace Storey Putnam's *Bye-Lo Baby,* representing a three-day-old baby, became a tremendous success. So many of the dolls were sold that it was actually called the "Million Dollar Baby." The *Bye-Lo* bisque heads were made in Germany by Alt, Beck & Gottschalck; Kling & Co., Hertel Schwab & Co. and J.D. Kestner. Those with mold numbers 1369 and 1372 were probably made by A.B.G. The cloth bodies were made by K & K Toy Co. of New York and George Borgfeldt distributed the dolls. By 1925, all of the German porcelain factories were making infant dolls.

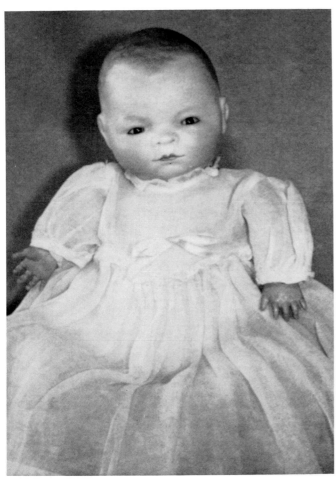

Illustration 223. Grace Storey Putnam's *Bye-Lo Baby.* She has a bisque head with flange neck on a marked cloth body with curved legs and celluloid hands. She was such the rage that people stood in line for hours to buy her. *Carter Craft Dollhouse Collection. Photograph by Thelma Bateman.*

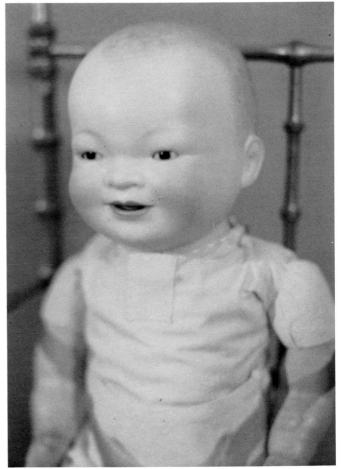

Illustration 224. A very rare smiling version of the *Bye-Lo Baby. Becky Roberts Lowe Collection.*

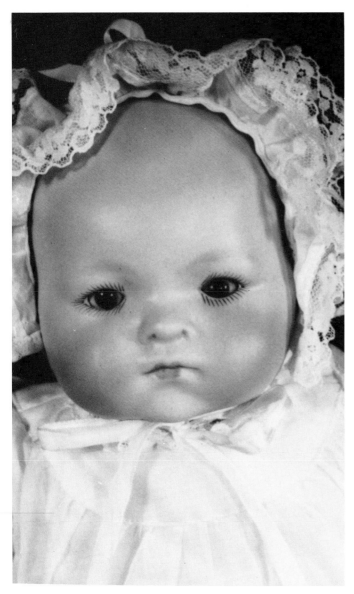

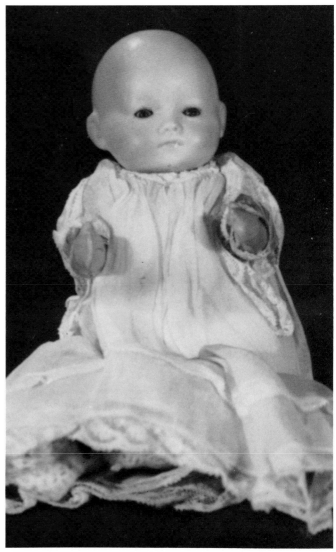

CLOCKWISE: Illustration 225. A beautiful baby, A.M. 341, some of which were marketed by Arranbee as *My Dream Baby*, seems to have been the chief competitor of the *Bye-Lo Baby*, judging by numbers found today. This baby has a flange neck on a cloth body. She is 16in (41cm) long. *H&J Foulke, Inc.*

Illustration 226. Armand Marseille made *Baby Phyllis* for the Baby Phyllis Doll Co. of Brooklyn, New York. She has a cloth body with composition hands, 11in (28cm) tall. *Emily Manning Collection.*

Illustration 227. Ernst Heubach of Köppelsdorf made several molds of newborn infants, but they are all difficult to find. This 9in (23cm) baby is mold 349. Other numbers to look for are 338, 339, 340 and 350. *H&J Foulke, Inc.*

RIGHT: Illustration 228. A large 16in (41cm) example of Amberg's *New Born Babe* which was reissued in 1924 with the success of the *Bye-Lo Baby*. Many heads carry the 1914 copyright date. *Richard Wright Collection.*

BOTTOM LEFT: Illustration 229. Hermann Steiner established his porcelain factory in 1920, after being in the toy business since 1911. This fretting baby with tiny glass eyes and open/closed mouth carries his H.S. mark. *Joyce Alderson Collection.*

BOTTOM RIGHT: Illustration 230. The Century Doll Co. of New York advertised in 1925 a series of bisque baby heads made by Kestner & Co. of Ohrdruf. This realistic baby carries the marks of both companies. *Thelma Bateman Collection. Photograph by Thelma Bateman.*

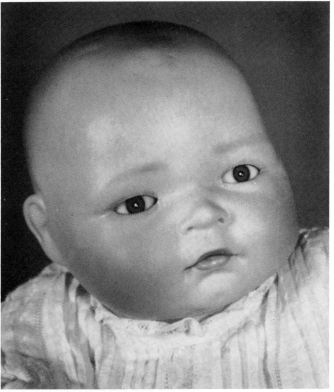

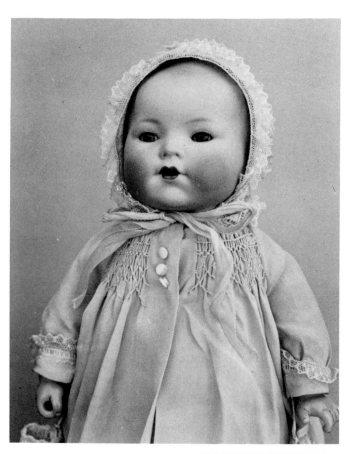

Illustration 231. Kämmer & Reinhardt made only a few models of infant dolls. This baby is mold number 8173 and was made in Simon & Halbig's porcelain factory. It is a rare doll and is 14in (36cm) long. *Clendenien Collection.*

BELOW: Illustration 232. Schoenau & Hoffmeister Porzellanfabrik Burggrub made this 13in (33cm) rare pouty baby, a favorite with collectors. It is incised with "S" "PB" in a star and "H." *Mary Lou Rubright Collection.*

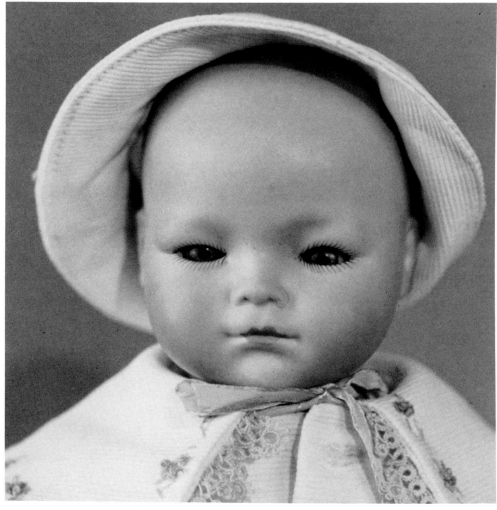

III. All-Bisque Dolls

Dolls that are made completely of bisque are favorites of many collectors. Being such fragile playthings, it is really amazing that so many of them have survived in perfect condition with all of their original parts. The large 8-10in (20-25cm) dolls, particularly, must have been quite hazardous to play with. It seems the smaller the doll, the less likely it is to have damage. If there is a problem with the tiny ones, it is often lost limbs. When buying all-bisque dolls, it is important to verify that all of the parts are correct and none have been inappropriately replaced.

The majority of all-bisque dolls were made in Germany, but a few were made in France. German porcelain factories which produced large numbers of all-bisque dolls were Hertwig & Co., Kestner & Co., Simon & Halbig and Limbach Porzellanfabrik.

Small all-bisque dolls are favorites, also, because of the wide variety of types available from early frozen dolls of the 1860s to tiny pretinted bisque characters of the 1930s. Small dolls are popular, too, because they do not take as much space to display attractively as do larger dolls. A portion of a china cabinet, top of an end table or corner of a bookcase can hold a large group of small dolls and accessories. Scenes assembled around a focus of small dolls are particularly appealing.

Fortunately, for today's collectors who are partial to miniatures, small dolls have been favorites of children for more than 100 years. Little girls have always liked tiny dolls, just large enough to hold in their hands, or slip in their pockets to take riding in the car, to church, school or anywhere else they could possibly go.

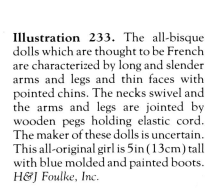

Illustration 233. The all-bisque dolls which are thought to be French are characterized by long and slender arms and legs and thin faces with pointed chins. The necks swivel and the arms and legs are jointed by wooden pegs holding elastic cord. The maker of these dolls is uncertain. This all-original girl is 5in (13cm) tall with blue molded and painted boots. *H&J Foulke, Inc.*

FAR RIGHT: Illustration 234. This 5½in (14cm) tall French all-bisque girl is all original with the further desirable characteristic of bare feet, a rarely found feature. *H&J Foulke, Inc.*

Illustration 235. Hertwig & Co., although founded in 1864, did not mention dolls as part of their production until 1884. This large porcelain factory in Katzhutte, Thüringia, produced china and bisque shoulder heads and parts as well as all-bisque dolls. They employed about 900 workers, nearly the whole town. This 6in (15cm) boy in an orange suit of about 1910 was a popular model. He has wire jointed arms and came in a variety of sizes. *H&J Foulke, Inc.*

Illustration 236. Another Hertwig boy, this one 7in (18cm) tall, in a white suit with green and brown trim, also of about 1910. He is wire-jointed at the shoulders. The quality of the Hertwig dolls is generally very good. *H&J Foulke, Inc*

124

Illustration 237. This 6in (15cm) girl has several desirable characteristics: a swivel neck and long blue stockings up over her knees. She appears to be a Simon & Halbig doll like their mold 886. The very fragile hands which stick out are indicative of S & H all-bisque dolls. She is a wonderful all-original doll. *H&J Foulke, Inc.*

Illustration 238. It is unusual to find an all-bisque Kämmer & Reinhardt child, but here is an all-original model with sleeping eyes, open mouth and swivel neck, as well as long white hose. This doll is 5in (13cm) tall. *H&J Foulke, Inc.*

Illustration 239. This French-type brown all-bisque is a very rare model. She has a swivel neck with pegged jointed shoulders and hips. Not only does she have desirable bare feet, but she has molded arm and leg bracelets. She is 4½in (12cm) tall. *H&J Foulke, Inc.*

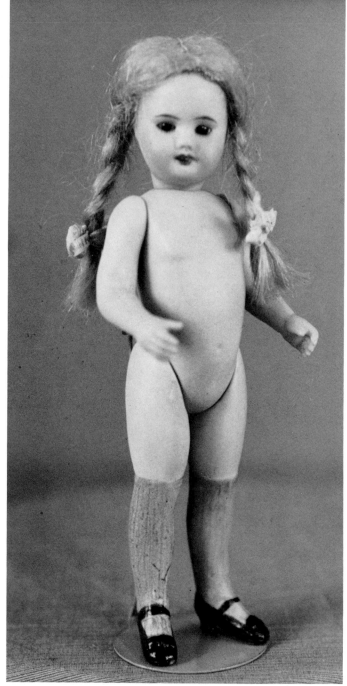

RIGHT: Illustration 240. A rarely found French all-bisque marked "S.F.B.J." She is 6¾in (17cm) tall with sleeping eyes, open mouth with molded teeth, and swivel neck. Her long over-the-knee stockings are gold. *H&J Foulke, Inc.*

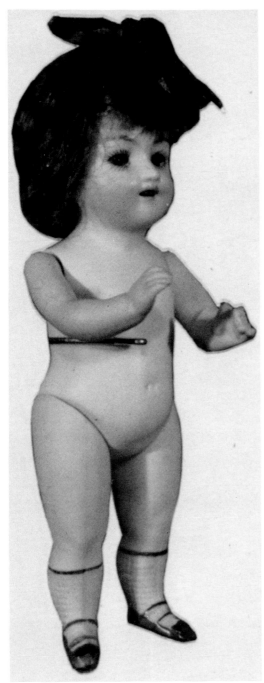

Illustration 242. It is fairly unusual to find a molded hair doll with a swivel neck, such as this one. She also has a molded bow at the back of her head and wears her original dress. She is just 4in (10cm) tall, German made. *H&J Foulke, Inc.*

Illustration 241. Kestner & Co. porcelain factory of Ohrdruf made quite a few all-bisque dolls of very good quality bisque. Their footwear was also well designed and this girl has shirred white hose, blue garters and brown two-strap shoes with pompons. She has a character-type face with open mouth and upper teeth and two deep side dimples. She is mold number 150, 7in (18cm) tall, with the chubby torso and limbs typical of the sturdy German all-bisque dolls. A similar doll is offered in the *Marshall Field & Co. 1914 Catalog. H&J Foulke, Inc.*

Illustration 243. A child of the 1920s, this 3in (8cm) boy has a small hole through his arm to tie the string which is attached to his bisque elephant. The paint on these immobile figures from the 1920s is not fired in, so it wears off easily. He is marked "Germany." *H&J Foulke, Inc.*

LEFT: **Illustration 244.** The all-bisque bathing beauty dolls are very sought after by collectors. These beautifully modeled and decorated dolls were made by nearly all of the Thüringian (Germany) porcelain factories. These fine quality ladies have painted facial features and stylish mohair wigs. The beauties came in a variety of standing, sitting and lying poses, often with lace or knit bathing suits and head scarves. Heights about 3 to 8in (8-20cm). *Private Collection.*

BELOW LEFT: **Illustration 245.** Jeanne I. Orsini patented her all-bisque character dolls in 1919 and 1920. This cute smiling character is *DiDi* in the 5in (13cm) size. She has tiny glass eyes and open/closed mouth with painted teeth. Characteristic of the Orsini dolls is the raised index finger on the right hand. This is very vulnerable and is often broken off when they are found today. The legs have long white over-the-knee stockings and black low one-strap shoes. The dolls had a paper label on the chest, and were incised on the back with "JIO." *H&J Foulke, Inc.*

BELOW RIGHT: **Illustration 246.** A companion doll is Jeanne Orsini's *MiMi*, shown in the 5in (13cm) size. She has a round open/closed mouth with painted teeth, also the same characteristic raised right index finger. *H&J Foulke, Inc.*

Continued on page 137.

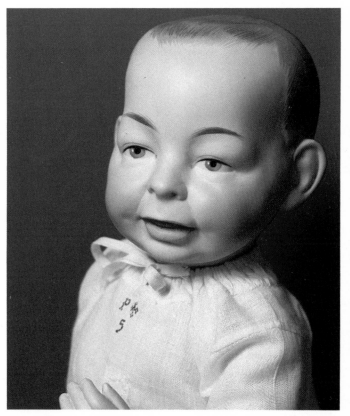

16in (41cm) all-bisque character baby, incised "229.36," with excellent modeling, not only in the face, but in the body detail, as well. Very rarely is an all-bisque doll found in this wonderful large size. *Joanna Ott Collection.*

FAR RIGHT: 7in (18cm) all-bisque doll with molded hair and fancy bonnet and painted facial features. She is a very nice quality doll with pale tinting. Her arms are wire-jointed, but her hips are stiff. *H&J Foulke, Inc.*

8½in (22cm) all-bisque child with swivel neck attributed to Kestner & Co. She has her original blonde mohair wig over a plaster pate, tiny brown almond-shaped sleeping eyes and pouty closed mouth. She is incised "111." These barefoot dolls are very desirable. *Jan Foulke Collection.*

7½in (19cm) unmarked all-bisque child with swivel neck. This exceptional doll has cobalt eyes and feathered blonde eyebrows. *Roberts Collection.*

22in (56cm) china head lady doll with hairdo referred to as "Jenny Lind" with hair fluffed out at sides and pulled back into a bun in a style of the 1860s. *Joanna Ott Collection.*

19in (48cm) china head lady doll with hairdo referred to as "Adelina Patti" in a style of the 1870s. *Joanna Ott Collection.*

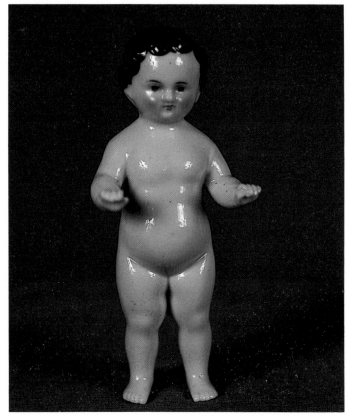

A blonde-haired china head with curly bangs and molded and painted ribbon band of the 1880s. *H&J Foulke, Inc.*

A 5½in (14cm) bathing doll or so-called *Frozen Charlotte* with short hairdo to represent a child. This is a very chubby doll with very good modeling detail. *H&J Foulke, Inc.*

A beautiful, large 23in (58cm) Sonneberg Taufling in exceptional condition. *Private Collection.*

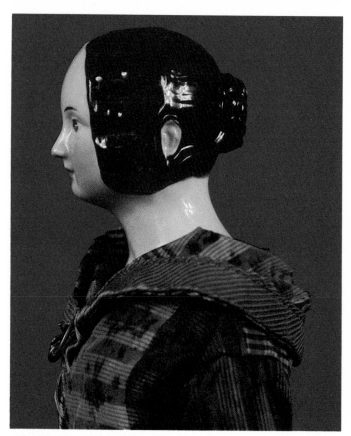

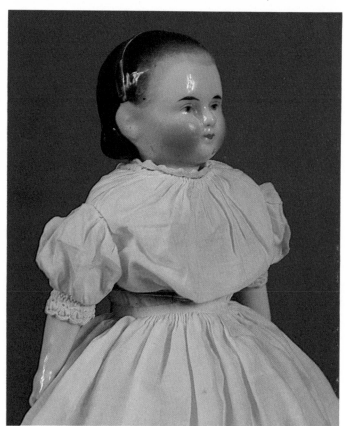

A lovely 19in (48cm) china head lady with brown hair and pink complexion dating from the 1840s. *Private Collection.*

A 10½in (27cm) china head child with molded ribbon in her hair and china hips and limbs. *Private Collection.*

A 16in (41cm) black-haired china lady with brown inset glass eyes of the 1850s. Her hairdo is the so-called Greiner-style with center part and hair smooth to ears and short curls in back. *Private Collection.*

A black-haired china head lady of the 1840s with an unusual long curl hair style. *Private Collection.* (For other china head dolls, see pages 141 to 154.)

A 24in (61cm) papier-mâché shoulder head doll on a French kid body of the 1840s. She has an open mouth with upper and lower bamboo teeth. *Private Collection.* (See page 158 for more information on this type of doll.)

FAR RIGHT: A Sonneberg Täufling with papier-mâché head, shoulder plate, lower arms, hands, lower torso, lower legs and feet. The rest of his body is cloth. He has glass eyes and painted hair. Sonneberg doll makers produced this type of doll beginning about 1852. *H&J Foulke, Inc.*

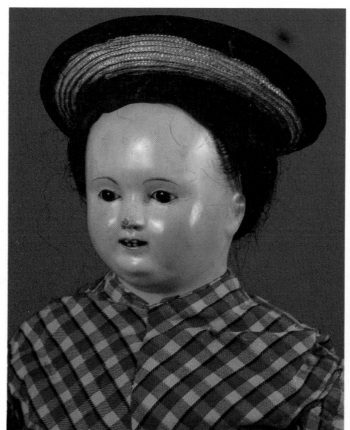

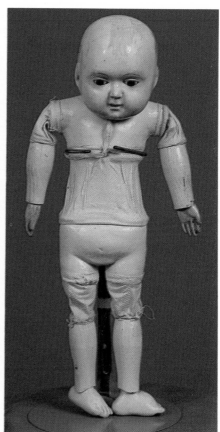

A 10in (25cm) Sonneberg Täufling of papier-mâché and cloth with original clothing. *Private Collection.*

A very rare 12in (31cm) china head doll wearing molded white bonnet with pink trim. *Private Collection.*

This is an early and rare pair of Japanese papier-mâché play dolls called the three-bend type which bend at the knee and can kneel. They are wearing original clothing and are just 8-9in (20-23cm) tall. *Private Collection.*

BELOW: This papier-mâché shoulder head doll with a hairdo of the 1850s is unmarked, but she is a very desirable Pre-Greiner doll with painted eyes. *Private Collection.* (See page 158 for another Pre-Greiner doll.)

Two large papier-mâché shoulder heads made by Ludwig Greiner in Philadelphia, bearing his 1858 label. Hair styles are similar, but not identical. *Joanna Ott Collection.*

A rare 1858 label Ludwig Greiner doll with inset glass eyes. All original, she is 25in (64cm) tall. *Private Collection.*

BELOW: A large 34in (86cm) Ludwig Greiner papier-mâché shoulder head with unusual short hairdo and barely smiling mouth. *Private Collection.* (For other Ludwig Greiner dolls, see page 161.)

BOTTOM RIGHT: This 16in (41cm) Munich Art Doll has a composition head with molded hair. He is all original on a jointed composition body. *Private Collection.* (See page 160 for other Munich Art Dolls.)

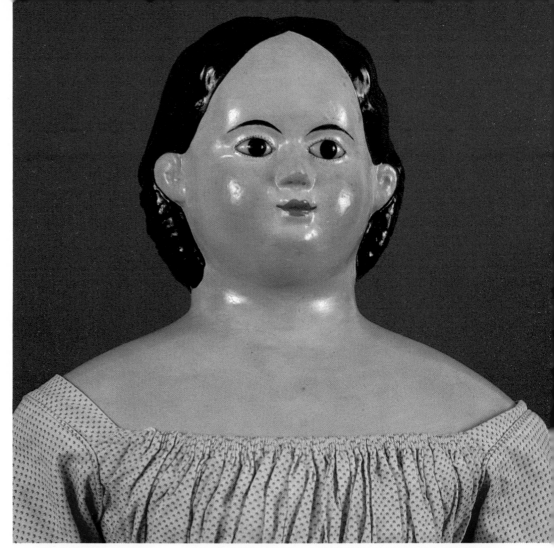

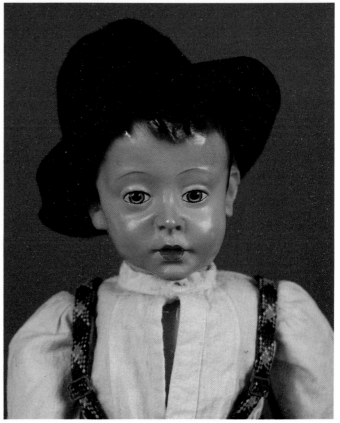

135

By about 1840, the lady type papier-mâché heads with fancy hairdos were giving way to a new type of head with the look of a child. These had round faces with painted or sometimes glass eyes, short thick necks, and short black windblown hair with wispy brush marks around the face. Some of these dolls with side-parted hair were dressed as men. And, of course, some were dressed as women, but the heads were advertised as "child heads" which was their primary purpose. This child papier-mâché is 17in (43cm) tall. *Private Collection.*

TOP LEFT: A pair of German-made googlies with papier-mâché faces and round glass eyes. They have cloth bodies and are all original. These novelties were produced in the 1911-1914 era by various companies under trade names, such as *Little Bright Eyes* and *Hug Me Kiddies.* H&J Foulke, Inc.

LEFT: A group of three early German papier-mâché shoulder heads with black molded hairdos. All have kid bodies with wooden limbs. *Joanna Ott Collection.* (See page 157 for other early papier-mâché ladies.)

Continued from page 128.

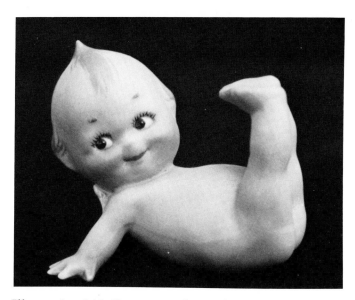

Illustration 248. *Kewpies* were designed in all sorts of positions and wearing parts of many different costumes and performing many household acts. There are over 100 variations in action *Kewpies*. This little 2½in (6cm) long fellow is catching up on fitness exercise. *H&J Foulke, Inc.*

Illustration 247. Rose O'Neill's whimsical and playful *Kewpie* dolls are practically irresistible, as shown by the fact that *Kewpies* have been on the new doll market continuously since their introduction in 1913. All-bisque *Kewpies* were made in numerous German factories, including Kestner & Co. This 6in (15cm) *Kewpie* is rare because of his jointed hips as most all-bisque standing *Kewpies* have pedestal legs. He still retains his original paper label on his chest. The outspread fingers (starfish-type) are typical for *Kewpie* dolls. *H&J Foulke, Inc.*

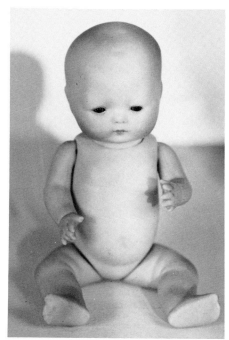

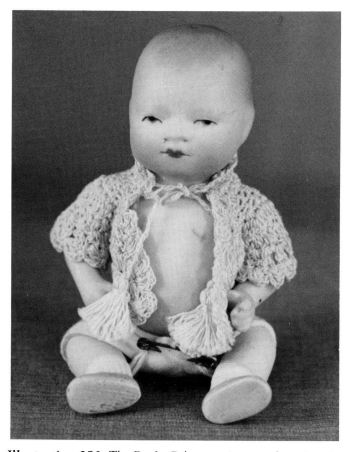

Illustration 249. The E. I. Horsman Co. of New York copyrighted their *Tynie Baby* in 1924 and had the bisque heads for the larger dolls and the small all-bisque dolls made in Germany. Of course, this was competition for Borgfeldt's *Bye-Lo Baby*. *Tynie Baby* was designed by Bernard Lipfert. 9in (23cm) tall, he has glass eyes and a swivel neck, making him a very desirable little doll. *Richard Wright Collection.*

Illustration 250. The *Bye-Lo Baby* came in several versions in all-bisque variations. This 4½in (12cm) fellow has molded white socks and pink booties. This painted-eye version also came with pink booties or barefooted. *H&J Foulke, Inc.* (For more information on *Bye-Lo Babies*, see page 119.)

137

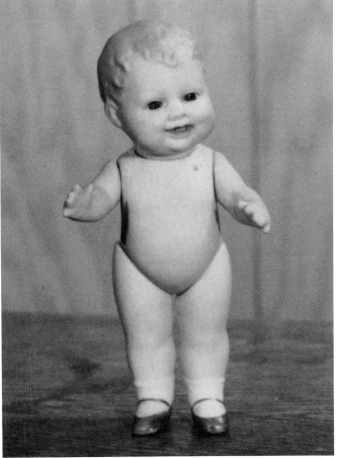

TOP LEFT: Illustration 251. Tiny all-bisque *Bye-Lo Babies* even came in variations with glass eyes and wigs. This 6½in (17cm) baby has glass eyes and swivel neck. The centimeter size numbers (the numbers after the hyphen) on the torso, arms and legs should match. *H&J Foulke, Inc.*

TOP RIGHT: Illustration 252. *Scootles* is another Rose O'Neill doll, this one from about 1925. He has the remains of his paper chest label and is marked on his feet "Scootles" and "Germany." This beautifully modeled version is 7½in (19cm) tall. *Becky Roberts Lowe Collection.*

LEFT: Illustration 253. Georgene Averill's *Bonnie Babe* was registered in 1926. The all-bisque dolls were possibly made by Alt, Beck & Gottschalck. This darling 5½in (14cm) doll has molded hair, glass eyes and smiling mouth. His chubby body has a swivel neck and molded white socks and blue strap shoes. *Private Collection.*

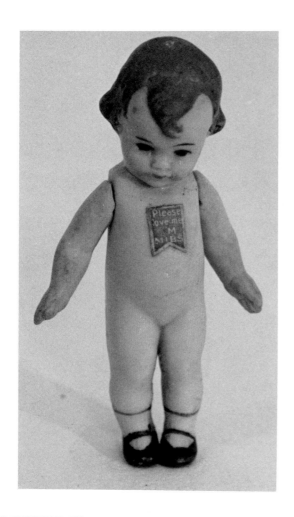

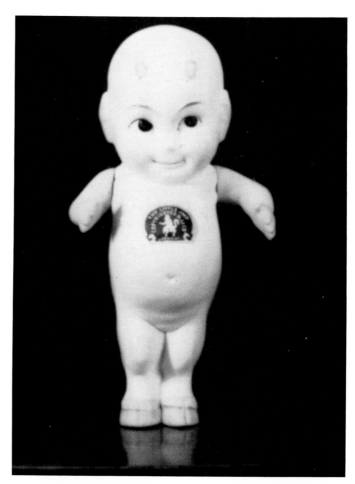

CLOCKWISE: Illustration 254. *Mibs* was designed by Hazel Drukker and copyrighted in 1921. Louis Amberg Co. had this all-bisque version made in Germany. She still retains her original paper label which reads: "Please//Love me//I'm//MIBS." She is made of pink pretinted bisque with molded and painted brown shoes. *H&J Foulke, Inc.*

Illustration 255. Many novelty dolls came out during the popularity of the *Kewpie* dolls. This one with molded horns and hoofs is "The Little Imp," copyrighted by B. Illfelder & Co. of New York and made in Germany. He is 7in (18cm) tall. *Richard Wright Antiques.*

Illustration 256. "The Medic" must have come out in the World War I era. His molded uniform is quite well done and he is carrying his medical bag. The Red Cross symbol is on his hat, arm band and bag. He is 4in (10cm) tall. *H&J Foulke, Inc.*

Illustration 257. Kate Jordan was the designer of the *Happifats* dolls. They were registered by George Borgfeldt in 1913. The pictured dolls are 4in (10cm) tall and are marked "©" which indicates that they are German. The girl's dress is light blue shaded with a darker blue; her sash and shoes are pink. The boy's pants are brown, his jacket dark green. The cute character faces have smiling mouths with painted teeth. *Richard Wright Collection.*

Illustration 258. This is "Freshie," the *Happifat* Baby, wearing a white molded suit. Just 3½in (9cm) tall, he is a very hard-to-find doll. *H&J Foulke, Inc.*

Illustration 259. *Little Annie Rooney* dates from 1925. She is all-bisque with moving arms only. Her black jacket and green skirt are nicely molded and she still retains her original yellow yarn hair and red felt cap. Across her shoulders she is marked "Germany." The rest of her markings are on her skirt. The doll was designed by Joseph Kallus from the Jack Collins comic strip. She is 4in (10cm) high. *H&J Foulke, Inc.*

IV. China Dolls

Although the Chinese had known the secrets of making porcelain for at least 1000 years before, it was only in the early 1700s that German manufacturers developed a formula for hard porcelain. The famous Meissen factory (K.P.M.) was the first to produce porcelain. The important ingredient in porcelain is kaolin or clay, available in varying qualities and consistencies in various parts of the world. Baking the clay mixture in kilns to intense degrees of heat actually makes the porcelain. As the demand for porcelain products rose, more factories were established, each with their own formulas revolving around the important kaolin. Many of these were in Thüringian forests, which offered ideal conditions for the manufacture of porcelain. There was wood from the forests to fuel the furnaces, plenty of cheap labor and the right kaolin. Since Thüringia (including Sonneberg and Waltershausen) was already a toy-making center, it seems only natural for some entrepreneur to conceive the idea of making dolls and doll heads of porcelain. It appears that the idea probably developed as a result of figurine production, and that the first china heads were intended as craft projects for adults, rather than as toys for children. Although china head dolls were probably produced as early as the mid-1700s, it was not until the 1840s that they began to be produced in greater numbers.

China is a glazed or glossy porcelain, as opposed to bisque which has a matte finish. Made in a simple two-piece mold, the early china head dolls had molded hairdos, for the most part. The kaolin mixture was rolled out like dough and hand-pressed into the molds. The hand-pressed heads can be recognized because of the varying thickness of the head and the inside indentations of utensils, sponges or hands which pressed the porcelain dough into the mold. By 1870, some of the German heads were being poured, as a method had been developed whereby the kaolin mixture could be liquified and poured into the molds. This method left the inside of the head smooth and the thickness of the head the same throughout. By 1890, virtually all of the German doll heads were poured.

Most of the china heads and limbs before 1880 were apparently sold individually and the buyers supplied their own bodies, a few commercially made, but most made at home. This explains why some of these dolls are found on ungainly out-of-proportion bodies. Later china heads were on well-proportioned bodies with varying qualities of china arms and legs. Some of the bodies were interesting with sewn-on corsets and stockings, even leather boots. The china legs offer a wide variety of colors of boots and make a very interesting study.

In addition to china head and limb dolls, porcelain factories were turning out lots of all-porcelain dolls, generally referred to as "bathing dolls" as they could be played with in water and many of the light porcelain dolls could float. These dolls are also called *Frozen Charlottes* by collectors.

Unfortunately, the majority of china head and bathing dolls are unmarked and porcelain factories responsible for the dolls are unknown. Some of the very early heads are marked with Meissen (K.P.M.) and Royal Copenhagen ciphers. Some of the later dolls are marked with known Alt, Beck & Gottschalck mold numbers or the "K" in Bell symbol of Kling & Co. However, most are unmarked and unidentifiable, such as those from Kestner & Co., Bähr & Pröschild, Goebel and Hertwig (except for the pet name heads from Hertwig). Many other porcelain factories made china head dolls, such as Kloster Veilsdorf and Schlaggenwald, but their names are not yet very familiar to most doll collectors.

By the 1870s, china head dolls were losing in popularity to bisque head dolls, although china heads continued to be made in large numbers through the 1880s into the 1890s. They were still being made in small numbers in the 1920s. It is amazing that this type of doll stayed in production for nearly 100 years.

A. French China Head Ladies

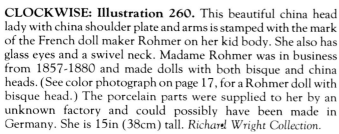

CLOCKWISE: Illustration 260. This beautiful china head lady with china shoulder plate and arms is stamped with the mark of the French doll maker Rohmer on her kid body. She also has glass eyes and a swivel neck. Madame Rohmer was in business from 1857-1880 and made dolls with both bisque and china heads. (See color photograph on page 17, for a Rohmer doll with bisque head.) The porcelain parts were supplied to her by an unknown factory and could possibly have been made in Germany. She is 15in (38cm) tall. *Richard Wright Collection.*

Illustration 261. The French china ladies have a very soft flesh-colored complexion tint, as compared to the stark whiteness of many of the German china heads with molded hair. The glass inset eyes are almond-shaped, long and narrow, with short dark painted eyelashes. This doll, on a gusseted kid body, is 20in (51cm) tall. *Private Collection.*

Illustration 262. This 16in (40cm) French china head lady has very narrow glass inset eyes with light eyebrows which consist of tiny individual brush strokes. Her shoulder head with stiff neck is mounted on a body completely of kid. *Joyce Alderson Collection.*

OPPOSITE PAGE: Illustration 263. This 14in (36cm) French china head lady with the mark of Mme. Rohmer on her body has lovely blue painted eyes enhanced by a dark upper lid eyeliner and long lightly painted upper and lower lashes. She has a swivel neck of the flat flange type found on many Rohmer dolls. *Pearl D. Morley Collection.*

B. German China Head Dolls

RIGHT and BELOW: **Illustrations 264 and 265.** Certainly one of the aristocrats of china head dolls, this wonderful lady with molded brown hair is a rare and desirable model. Her complexion is pink-toned. The profile view shows her well modeled features and extremely long neck. These types of dolls were made about 1840 in Germany by the factory at Meissen (K.P.M.) and in Denmark at Royal Copenhagen. The pictured lady is 18in (46cm) tall. *Richard Wright Antiques.* (See page 132 for a color photograph of a doll with this hairdo.)

RIGHT: **Illustration 266.** A china head with black short hair and brush strokes at the temples usually used as a boy or man dates from about 1840-1850. The body is cloth with leather arms. *Grace Dyar Antique Dolls.*

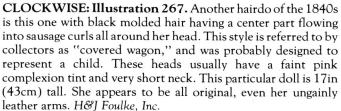

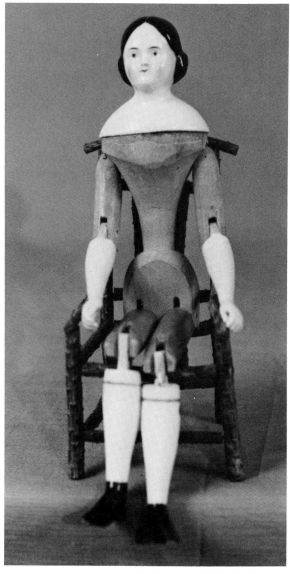

CLOCKWISE: Illustration 267. Another hairdo of the 1840s is this one with black molded hair having a center part flowing into sausage curls all around her head. This style is referred to by collectors as "covered wagon," and was probably designed to represent a child. These heads usually have a faint pink complexion tint and very short neck. This particular doll is 17in (43cm) tall. She appears to be all original, even her ungainly leather arms. *H&J Foulke, Inc.*

Illustration 268. This large pink-toned head has less detail in the hair molding than others of this style. Her face is quite round and her eye sockets are very deeply molded. *H&J Foulke, Inc.*

Illustration 269. Some of the 1840s china head dolls came on peg-wooden bodies with china arms and legs. This 14in (36cm) model has a pink tinted complexion and plain hairdo of the 1840s. *H&J Foulke, Inc.*

Illustration 270. The tiny china head dolls come in nearly as large a variety of hairdos as do the larger ones. This 6½in (17cm) lady has hair combed back into a bun with tiny brush marks showing at the sides. She is totally original. *H&J Foulke, Inc.*

BELOW: Illustration 271. Rarely are the German molded hair china dolls found with glass eyes. This black-haired doll with clusters of tight curls and white center part dates from about 1850. Her glass eyes are enhanced by one-stroke eyebrows and painted upper and lower eyelashes. She also has a molded upper eyelid. The shoulders are very sloped and the shoulder plate is deep. *Grace Dyar Antique Dolls.*

OPPOSITE PAGE: Illustration 272. This lady, with the same hairdo as shown in the previous illustration, has painted brown eyes. This is fairly unusual as most china head dolls have blue eyes. She is 16in (41cm) tall. *Pearl D. Morley Collection.* (See color photograph on page 132 for a glass-eyed china lady with a molded "Greiner-style" hairdo.)

Illustration 273. Dating from the 1850s are the china infants with china midsections. Apparently, this style of Sonneberg *Täufling* was developed when Edmund Lindner brought a Japanese doll back to Sonneberg from the London Exposition of 1851. Most of the Sonneberg *Täuflings* were of papier-mâché (See color illustrations on page 134); rarely is a china model found. This 9in (23cm) child has a flange swivel neck on a shoulder plate, china arms, midsection and legs. The rest of the body is cloth. His hair is painted black. *Louise Ceglia Antique Dolls.*

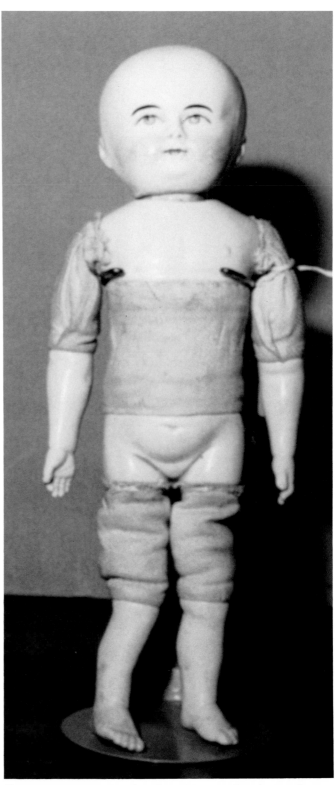

Illustration 274. Another 9in (23cm) infant but with quite different modeling. *Grace Dyar Antique Dolls.* (See page 132 for a china head child with a molded band in her hair.)

Illustration 275. This style of black-haired china head with a fairly plain hairdo having a smooth crown and short curls all around the head was made in abundance with quite a few variations. There must have been a large number of porcelain factories producing them. They date from about 1860. This large 27in (69cm) lady is quite unusual because she has a molded necklace. *Dr. Carole Stoessel Zvonar Collection.*

Illustration 276. In the 1860s, the snood became popular and fashionable. Not only did it make the hair more manageable, but it could also be very decorative. This lady has a snood with a white ruffled border and a cluster of grapes at the top. *H&J Foulke, Inc.*

149

TOP LEFT: Illustration 277. A lady with lovely long black hair and brush strokes around her forehead wearing a molded gold snood enclosing the lower part of her hair. She is 12in (31cm) tall. *Coleman Collection. Photograph by Thelma Bateman.*

LEFT: Illustration 278. A lovely 17in (43cm) lady with molded snood from the 1860s. She also has molded bows at the side of her head. *Grace Dyar Antique Dolls.*

TOP RIGHT: Illustration 279. This lovely black-haired china head lady from the 1860s not only has an unusual hairdo, she also has the desirable feature of pierced ears. She is all original, also. *Grace Dyar Antique Dolls.*

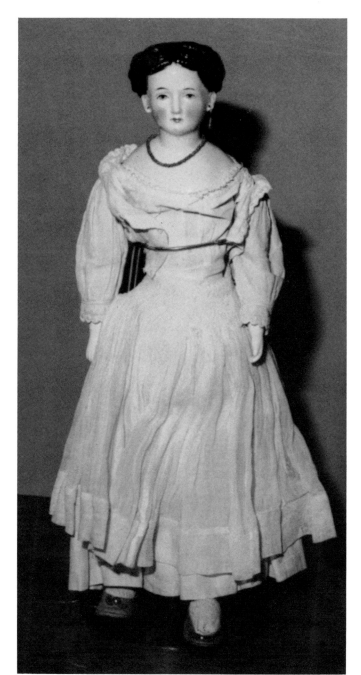

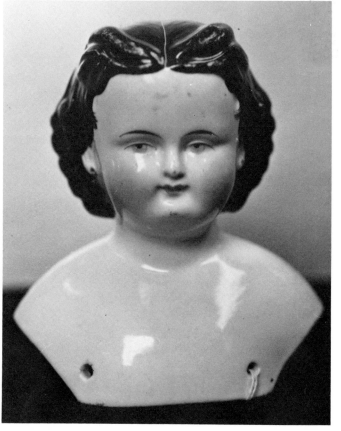

CLOCKWISE: Illustration 280. Another black-haired china head lady from the 1860s with pierced ears. Her hair is arranged in a fancy style high on her head. She is 18in (46cm) tall. *Grace Dyar Antique Dolls.*

Illustration 281. A large china head of the 1860s and 1870s with *cafe-au-lait* hair in a fancy style with long curls around the back and a hair band. *Grace Dyar Antique Dolls.*

Illustration 282. A plainer hairdo of the 1860s and 1870s is this black-haired model called "Adelina Patti" by collectors. *Grace Dyar Antique Dolls.* (For a color photograph of a doll with this hairdo, see page 130.)

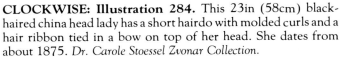

CLOCKWISE: Illustration 284. This 23in (58cm) black-haired china head lady has a short hairdo with molded curls and a hair ribbon tied in a bow on top of her head. She dates from about 1875. *Dr. Carole Stoessel Zvonar Collection.*

Illustration 285. A 20in (51cm) blonde-haired china head child from the 1880s with short wavy hair and exposed ears. *H&J Foulke, Inc.*

Illustration 286. Alt, Beck & Gottschalck porcelain factory near Ohrdruf, Thüringia, has recently been identified as the maker of a series of molded hair dolls in both china and bisque with mold numbers ranging from the 700s to the 1200s. In the 1880s, they made boy and girl heads, some with molded caps as well. The A.B.G. china lower arms are molded to above the elbow with nice hands and large separate thumbs. The lower legs have molded black boots with heels and a painted garter. This head is from mold 1000, called *Highland Mary* by collectors. This child has molded bangs with tiny brush strokes across her forehead to give the hair a natural look. This china head style also comes with blonde hair, as do many of the 1880s dolls. A.B.G. also made this style in bisque with blonde hair and sometimes glass eyes, as well. She is 19in (48cm) tall. *Emily Manning Collection.*

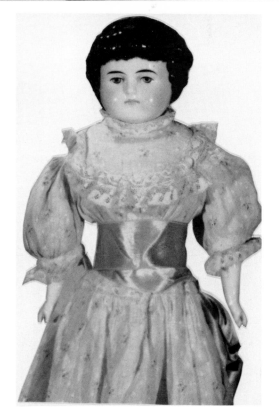

C. Bathing Dolls

Bathing dolls or so-called *Frozen Charlottes* are simply those china (and sometimes bisque) dolls which could be played with in water, either at the beach or at home, in the bathtub or in a pail of water. Bathing dolls are not jointed, but are all one piece. Ideally, the bathing dolls could float if they were made of fine light porcelain, but the cheaper and heavier dolls, of course, sank. The bathing doll was a staple product of the German porcelain factories for at least 60 years. In 1899, the smallest, cheapest ones offered by Butler Bros. were 85¢ per gross (144), intended to retail for 2¢ each. The large, well-decorated dolls, however, were much more expensive. Although most of the china bathing dolls are unmarked, factories which were known to have made them are Conta & Böhme and Kling & Co.

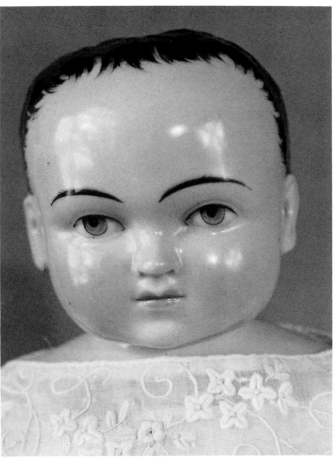

Illustration 289. This close-up view shows molded and black painted hair of a bathing doll which has paint brush strokes at his hairline to give a natural look. Even his eyebrows have tiny brush strokes along the top. The detail painting of the eye is excellent and even shows threading in the iris part. 15in (38cm) tall, he has an overall pink-toned complexion. *Mary Lou Rubright Collection.*

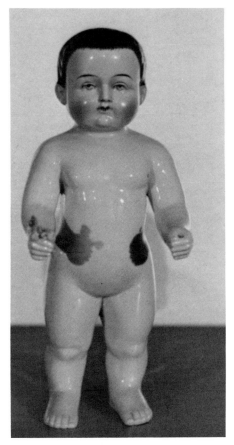

Illustration 288. A 13in (33cm) bathing doll with black painted hair and brush marks at his hairline to give a natural look. His face is flesh colored, but the rest of his body is white. Some bathing dolls are completely white on both face and body, and some are fully flesh colored on both face and body. *H&J Foulke, Inc.*

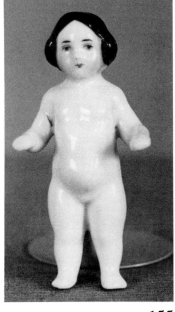

Illustration 290. A small 3in (8cm) china bathing doll with overall pink-tinted complexion and 1840s "covered wagon" hairdo. She is barefooted, although some bathing dolls have molded footwear. *H&J Foulke, Inc.* (See color photograph on page 130 for another style of bathing doll.)

V. Papier-Mâché and Composition Dolls

German doll makers were always experimenting with new materials which would produce a cheaper or more durable product. About 1805, toys and picture frames had begun to be manufactured from papier-mâché, which was nothing more than a mixture of old shredded and grated paper scraps with various portions of glue, ashes, flour, water, clay, chalk and coloring agents. When the substance dried and hardened, the articles were quite durable. About 1818, molds were developed and doll heads were made by pressing the wet papier-mâché into the molds; thus, mass production was possible. This gave great impetus to the Thüringian doll industry, and the Sonneberg factory owners were able to sell large quantities of papier-mâché doll heads and other articles. Sonneberg became the center of the German papier-mâché trade. Johann Müller was the first factory owner to produce doll heads, having the exclusive license in Sonneberg to produce the new doll heads. His factory later became known as Müller & Strassburger when he took in a partner. In 1822, he produced 58 types of doll heads. Meanwhile, across the mountains in Waltershausen, also a part of Thüringia, J.D. Kestner in 1822 received an exclusive license for making papier-mâché items for ten years. Unfortunately, these early papier-mâché dolls are unmarked and it is impossible to attribute them to specific makers.

The manufacture of papier-mâché doll heads and parts was largely carried out as a home industry. Complete households, including small children, were engaged in making parts. The gooey papier-mâché mass was pressed into molds. When the two halves of the head (front and back) were removed, they were glued together. The hair and features were painted; later the whole head was lacquered.

Different makers developed recipes of varying ingredients as they searched for the most durable papier-mâché. Later, heads were made with different additives, such as sawdust, and this mixture is usually referred to as composition, but it is really difficult to determine precisely whether some heads should be termed papier-mâché or composition. Heads of papier-mâché and composition were made in Germany for over 100 years, beginning in about 1818.

The German papier-mâché doll industry received a great boost in 1851 when Edmund Lindner brought a Japanese papier-mâché doll back to Sonneberg from the London Exhibition. Lindner, who was a *verlager* or exporter, gave the doll to a factory owner and asked him to make this type of doll. This type of doll with papier-mâché head, shoulder plate, lower torso and lower limbs with jointed wrists and ankles on a cloth body became so popular that the factories, the principal one of which was that of Heinrich Stier, were unable to deliver the dolls as fast as they were ordered. (See color photographs on page 133.) This "Sonneberg *Täufling*" appears to have been one of the first infant dolls. Original clothing consisted of a shift and sometimes bonnet. By 1857, the *Täuflings* had voice boxes patented by Christoph Motschmann and stamped with his trademark; hence, the confusion and reference to the dolls as made by Motschmann, when in fact, Motschmann patented only the voice boxes. In 1852, Heinrich Stier developed a method of coating the papier-mâché heads with a thin layer of wax to give the *Täuflings* a more lifelike appearance. A large verlager and exporter of *Täuflings* was Louis Lindner, who sold dolls which were made by a variety of factories and home industries.

A. German Papier-Mâché Dolls

CLOCKWISE: Illustration 291. A large 25in (64cm) lady with papier-mâché shoulder head, painted features and molded hair in a fancy style of the 1830s. *Richard Wright Collection.*

Illustration 292. This 15in (38cm) lady with papier-mâché shoulder head has a fancy black molded hairdo of the 1830s and painted facial features. She has a body typical of these early papier-mâché dolls which has a kid torso, kid upper arms and legs with wooden lower arms and legs. The body is stiff, not jointed, so the doll cannot sit down. *Joanna Ott Collection.*

Illustration 293. A molded hair papier-mâché lady, 12½in (32cm) tall, with a hair style of the 1840s. *Thelma Bateman Collection. Photograph by Thelma Bateman.*

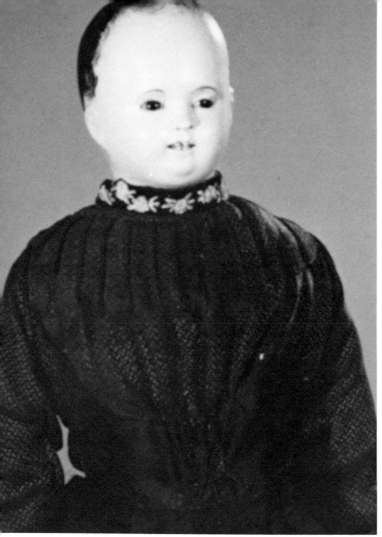

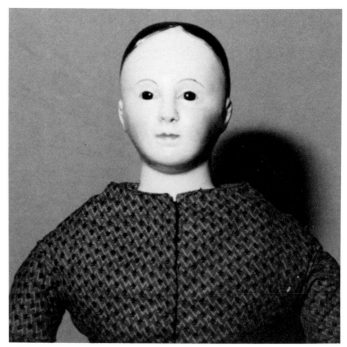

Illustration 295. A 23in (58cm) papier-mâché shoulder head lady of about 1840 with a lovely oval shaped face, inset glass eyes and closed mouth. She has a French-type kid body. *Elizabeth McIntyre Antique Dolls*

Illustration 294. This type of papier-mâché shoulder head from about 1840 is referred to as French-type because of her shapely kid body of white or pink leather. It is now felt by researchers that these heads were made in Sonneberg and sent to France where they were furnished with kid bodies, dressed and marketed as "French" dolls. These very desirable papier-mâché heads are bald with painted hair and generally, at one time, were furnished with a human hair wig which was nailed on. She has inset glass eyes and an open mouth with two upper and two lower bamboo teeth. Very few, if any, papier-mâché heads were actually made in France. *Private Collection.* (See color photograph on page 133 for another example of this type of doll.)

RIGHT: Illustration 296. This is a large 30in (76cm) papier-mâché shoulder head doll of the type referred to by collectors as "Pre-Greiner," as the style supposedly predates the 1858 patent of the Philadelphia manufacturer Ludwig Greiner. It has really not been determined who made these heads and whether or not they are German or American, but they are very desired by collectors of early dolls. This example has inset glass eyes and molded black hair in the style referred to as "Greiner." This type of head is found on a cloth body with leather arms. *Grace Dyar Antique Dolls.*

158

Illustration 297. Cuno & Otto Dressel of Sonneberg registered their "Holz-Masse" trademark for papier-mâché dolls in 1875. Actually, these dolls are more properly referred to as composition as these had less wood pulp and more of other ingredients in the composition. By the 1870s, the papier-mâché dolls, once so popular, were taking second place to the newer and more modern bisque dolls. Dressel was a long-established Sonneberg doll firm (1789) which not only had large factories of their own, but also bought goods from smaller factories and home workers. This composition shoulder head doll marked with the Dressel "Holzmasse" trademark has a serene face with painted eyes and a mohair wig. Her lower limbs are also composition, her blue boots being well modeled. Many dolls of this period have very elaborately molded footwear in a variety of colors: blue, red, green, brown, and so forth. She is 17in (43cm) tall and appears to be wearing original clothing. *Private Collection.*

Illustration 298. Many German firms were producing the composition head dolls in the 1870s and on. This one is of the type produced by Müller & Strassburger with typical blonde molded hair and painted eyes. She is 22in (56cm) tall on a cloth body with leather arms. *Private Collection.*

RIGHT: Illustration 299. This 21in (53cm) German papier-mâché shoulder head with black molded hair of the 1880s has multi-stroked eyebrows and detailed brush strokes to indicate individual strands of hair around her face. Her label is printed "Unbreakable// Heads//6000/1" but the maker remains unidentified. Some dolls of this type were made by Adolph Wislizenus. *Joanna Ott Collection.*

CLOCKWISE: Illustration 300. This type of papier-mâché or composition doll was referred to in contemporary catalogs as a *Patent Washable* doll and was very popular, inexpensive, in the period from 1890-1910. Quality varied greatly with the price, some dolls having a fine polished finish and some barely a thin coat of paint. This large 24in (61cm) doll has blue paperweight eyes and original mohair wig. She is wearing original inexpensive organdy clothes with lace trim. *H&J Foulke, Inc.*

Illustration 301. Many novelty dolls appear in contemporary catalogs of the 1890s, such as this black one with papier-mâché head and lower arms and legs. She was offered by Butler Bros. in the 1899 and 1910 catalogs as a "Nursing Doll" with a glass baby bottle. A 13in (33cm) doll was priced wholesale at $2.10 per dozen. Her body is cloth with a mechanism which opens her mouth when her chest is pressed. She is wearing her original cotton dress and lace-trimmed bonnet. *H&J Foulke, Inc.*

Illustration 302. Marion Kaulitz, a Munich artist, was the force behind the German doll reform movement of the early 1900s, which eventually caused the German doll industry to produce their totally original and most outstanding dolls — the character children. Kaulitz promoted realism in dolls; each was made after the likeness of a real child. The dolls were dressed in the country costumes as worn by the German children. The heads were of composition with hand-painted faces; some dolls were wigged, some had molded hair. The bodies were the same type of jointed composition as used with the German bisque head dolls. These three *Munich Art Dolls* are in original costumes. *Nancy Schwartz Blaisure Collection.*

160

B. American Papier-Mâché Dolls

In the United States, Philadelphia, Pennsylvania, seems to be the city which was the center for producing papier-mâché dolls. Probably the best known maker is Ludwig Greiner, who obtained his first doll patent in 1858, which was actually for an improvement on heads already being made by reinforcing them with cloth. So, obviously, he was making heads before this date, probably in the 1840s. Greiner was an immigrant from Germany, a member of an established doll-making family, who brought his doll-making skills with him. Other Philadelphia manufacturers of papier-mâché dolls were Lerch & Co., Lerch & Klag, Judge, Judge & Early, and Knell Bros.

(For other Greiner dolls, see color photographs on pages 134 and 135.)

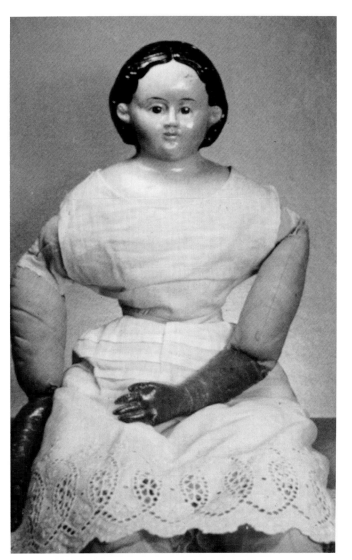

TOP RIGHT: Illustration 303. An early Ludwig Greiner doll with a papier-mâché shoulder head. Her black hair is molded in a style of the 1850s with exposed ears. She has painted eyes and a cloth body with leather lower arms and hands. She is 24in (61cm) tall. *Carter Craft Dollhouse Collection. Photograph by Thelma Bateman.*

TOP LEFT: Illustration 304. This 25in (64cm) Greiner shoulder head doll with the 1858 patent label has still another style of black molded hair among the wide variety offered by Greiner. The 1858 label dolls are favored by collectors over the later 1872 label. *Richard Wright Antiques.*

RIGHT: Illustration 305. This 26in (66cm) Greiner shoulder head doll with blonde molded hair has the 1872 patent label. At this time blonde and black-haired dolls were about evenly divided. *Coleman Collection. Photograph by Thelma Bateman.*

C. Oriental Papier-Mâché Dolls

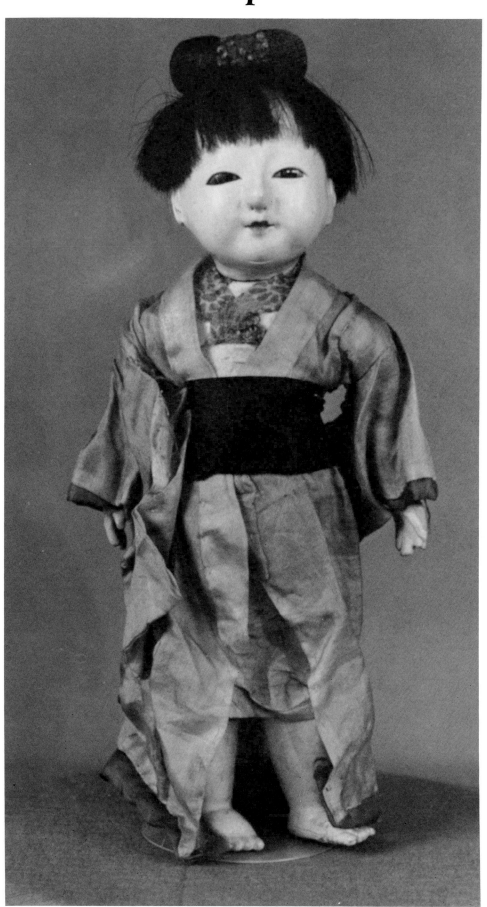

Illustration 306. The Japanese tradition of making papier-mâché dolls goes back hundreds of years. Many Japanese dolls are for decorative or ceremonial purposes, but this is an example of a *ningyo* or play doll. These models came as either boys or girls; some of the boys have painted hair. Dolls have papier-mâché heads, shoulder plates, lower torso and lower limbs. The midsection often contains a voice box and upper limbs are sometimes of paper. The doll shown is 10in (25cm) tall and dates from about 1900. She is wearing her original costume. *H&J Foulke, Inc.* (See page 134 for other Japanese papier-mâché dolls.)

VI. Wooden Dolls

Wooden dolls have been made through the known history of the doll and are still being made today. Some of the earliest commercial dolls, the English so-called "Queen Anne" dolls made as early as the late 17th century, were of carved wood. By the early 1700s, primitive wooden dolls were first produced in Sonneberg. These were simply turned on one piece of wood at first; soon the dolls were being painted and arms were added. Next, the dolls had bright red cheeks, tiny wooden noses and carved headgear. About 1780, Sonneberg was producing "Dancing Docken," tiny wooden dolls with bristles glued at the bottom which danced when placed on a slightly vibrating surface. By the late 18th Century, large numbers of wooden dolls were being made in Sonneberg, Germany, and the Grödner Tal in Austria. By 1800, some of these wooden dolls showed wonderful detail in carved features and elaborate hairdos involving braids, curls, combs and hair ornaments, even painted spit curls and earrings. Many carved wooden dolls even had a waist joint. J.D. Kestner of Waltershausen was one of the known makers of wooden dolls in 1820.

In the 1911 catalog of the Albert Schoenhut Co. of Philadelphia, it is noted that "Primitive Wooden Dolls were already made by Anton Wilhelm Schoenhut in Germany in 1796, and after his demise by his son Frederick Wilhelm Schoenhut from 1830 to 1860." Albert Schoenhut, who founded the Philadelphia factory which produced patented spring-jointed wooden dolls, was the youngest son of Frederick.

By about the mid 19th Century, papier-mâché, then china, and later bisque dolls took prominence over wooden dolls, but the latter continued to be made, primarily by German doll factories. In 1911, some German companies were advertising wood character dolls. French department store catalogs from the early 20th Century offered *Bébés Tout en Bois*, dolls all of wood. At this time Swiss craftsmen were hand-carving lovely jointed wooden dolls.

In the United States, wooden dolls were made by several Springfield, Vermont, factories in the 1870s and 1880s. The Albert Schoenhut factory in Philadelphia produced a large variety of patented wooden metal-jointed dolls from 1911 until the 1930s.

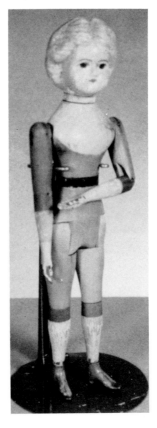 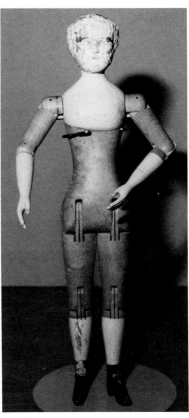

Illustration 307. Several companies making similar wooden dolls were located in Springfield, Vermont. This doll, formerly erroneously attributed to Mason & Taylor, is actually by the Jointed Doll Co. These dolls have a black band around the waist with the patent dates 1879, 1880 and 1882. The heads are composition over a wooden core; the hands and feet are metal. Dolls are usually 12in (31cm) tall. *Coleman Collection. Photograph by Thelma Bateman.*

FAR RIGHT: Illustration 308. Another Springfield, Vermont, factory, Co-operative Manufacturing Co., made wooden dolls from the 1873 patent of Joel Ellis, its president. These dolls have composition-over-wood heads, wood-jointed bodies and metal hands and feet. Heights were 12, 15 and 18in (31, 38 and 46cm). Some of the dolls were painted black. The pictured doll is 15in (38cm) tall. *Grace Dyar Antique Dolls.*

Illustration 309. An early 20in (51cm) English "Queen Anne" wooden doll with carved face and pupilless glass inset eyes with painted dotted eyelashes. She has a wooden body and is all original. *Richard Wright Collection.* (For a color photograph of a "Queen Anne" doll, see page 169.)

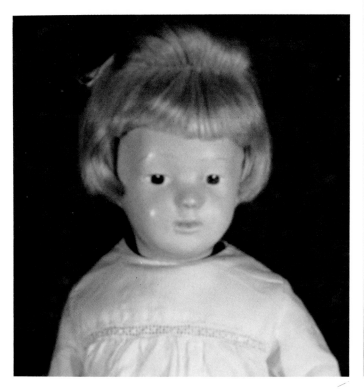

CLOCKWISE: **Illustration 310.** A 14in (36cm) all-wood girl by the Albert Schoenhut Co. of Philadelphia, Pennsylvania. Schoenhut patented their spring-jointed dolls in 1911, but the first year's business was disappointing and the company had to redesign the faces for 1912 and introduce additional sizes. (The first dolls were 16in [41cm]; in 1912, 14, 19 and 21in [36, 48 and 53cm] dolls were added.) This girl is model #312 with a pouty face and blonde mohair wig in bobbed style. *Roberts Collection.*

Illustration 311. This 19in (48cm) Schoenhut doll is model #314 with large painted eyes, chubby cheeks and pouty mouth. This model was available only in the 19in (48cm) size. She has a blonde mohair wig and is totally original. *H&J Foulke, Inc.* (See pages 169 and 170 for color photographs of other Schoenhut dolls.)

Illustration 312. The hand-carved Swiss wooden dolls from the early 20th Century are extremely well done and popular with collectors. This girl with carved face and hair is 14in (36cm) tall. She is jointed at neck, shoulders, elbows, hips and knees with painted shoes and stockings. Most of this type doll is dressed in regional costume. *Sheila Needle Collection. Photograph by Morton Needle.* (For another Swiss wooden doll see color photograph on page 170.)

VII. Wax Dolls

Wax had long been used for religious figures, portraiture and elaborate waxworks or tableaux, before it was adapted in the 19th Century as a material for making dolls. This seems to have developed mainly in London, England, where there were families, such as the Pierottis and Montanaris, who were very skilled in wax modeling.

With wooden dolls having degenerated to cheap workmanship, the moneyed people and the newly prosperous middle class were looking for a doll of high quality. The realism of the wax dolls along with their excellent modeling and detail seemed to fill the vacancy. It was simply a natural progression for the wax makers to proceed from portraits to dolls. Actually, it was probably the birth of Queen Victoria's many babies in the 1840s which spurred the demand for dolls. Mary Hillier feels that it was probably the Pierotti family that seized upon the idea of making wax models of the Royal Babies. These models were, of course, of great interest to the public, which clamored for their own copies of the Royal Children. Hence, a new type of expensive luxury doll developed. These beautiful wax models were blue-eyed with a small amount of soft blonde hair inserted in the wax scalp. The plump baby had a cloth body with realistically modeled wax arms and legs. These models were dressed in beautiful Victorian gowns with a lot of tucks, lace and ribbons, voluminous undergarments, embroidered booties and exquisite caps and silk carriage robes.

There is no doubt that the London makers produced the finest, most luxurious poured wax dolls. Their artistry and craftsmanship was superb. Firms in addition to Pierotti which followed the lead to create these dolls were Montanari, Meech, Marsh, Edwards, and Peck.

Heinrich Stier is credited with introducing wax dolls to Germany upon his return from the London Exhibition of 1851. He developed recipes for poured wax dolls that could resist extreme heat and cold and could resist nicks and scratches. It was his idea to put a wax coating on the papier-mâché Täuflings. Soon Germany was producing large numbers of the wax-over papier-mâché dolls. These dolls were popular until about 1890, by which time they were largely displaced by the bisque-head dolls.

A. English Wax Dolls

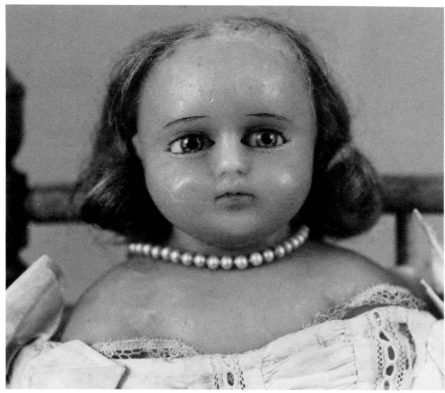

Illustration 313. An English doll with poured wax head, arms and legs and cloth body. She has hair inset into her wax scalp. She is 18in (46cm) tall and unmarked. *Joanna Ott Collection.*

Illustration 314. This 21in (53cm) English poured wax baby is by Lucy Peck. She is wearing her original clothing. *Betty Harms Collection.*

BELOW: Illustration 315. A 25in (64cm) doll with poured wax shoulder head and limbs after the style of Pierotti. Although, judging by her face, she was intended to be a child, many of this type are found dressed as young ladies. The bodies are adaptable to adult dressing as even the babies have nipped-in waists. *Pearl D. Morley Collection.* (For color photographs of poured wax dolls, see page 171.)

B. German Wax Dolls

Illustration 316. By 1875, the German factories were creating a large number of wax-over papier-mâché shoulder head dolls with various molded hairdos, some with molded ribbons, combs or other ornaments. Although some were of fine quality, many were made with just a thin coating of wax, and had very cheap gauze bodies with out-of-proportion limbs. Many had very interesting molded boots in a wide variety of styles. This 18in (46cm) wax-over shoulder head doll has molded blonde hair and inset glass eyes. *Richard Wright Antiques.*

Illustration 317. Here is another German wax-over papier-mâché shoulder head with blonde molded hair and bulgy dark pupilless glass eyes. She is 20in (51cm) tall. *Joanna Ott Collection.*

Continued on page 177.

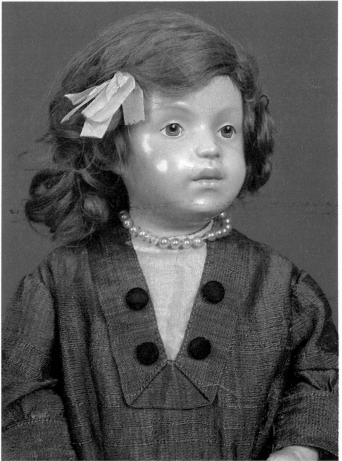

A large 18in (46cm) all-wood German doll with pegged joints dating about 1850, wearing original regional costume. *Joanna Ott Collection.*

TOP LEFT: A 16in (41cm) English wooden doll, so-called "Queen Anne" type with inset glass eyes dating about 1750. She has a peg-wooden body. *Private Collection.*

LEFT: A 19in (48cm) all-wood doll with metal spring joints by Albert Schoenhut of Philadelphia, patented in 1911. This doll is model #308, probably introduced in 1912, appearing in the 1915 Schoenhut catalog and still offered in 1924. She came with either curly (X) or bobbed (B) hair. She is all original. *Private Collection.*

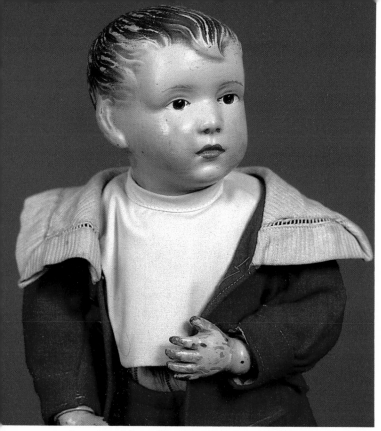

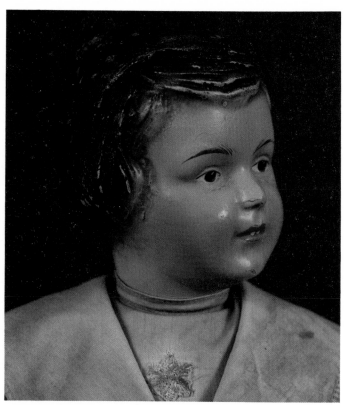

A Schoenhut boy with carved hair, model #204, probably introduced in 1912. He is 16in (41cm) tall and was offered in both the 1915 and 1916 catalogs. He is also known to exist in a 14in (36cm) size on a walking body. He was shown in the 1930 catalog when Schoenhut was offering dolls made from leftover parts. *Private Collection.*

A Schoenhut boy with carved hair, model #206, probably introduced in about 1913. He is offered in the Schoenhut 1915 and 1916 catalogs in this 19in (48cm) size only. He is all original. *Private Collection.*

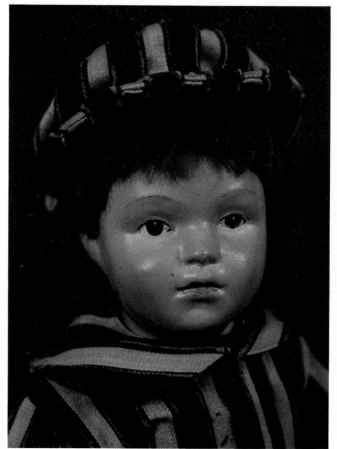

FAR LEFT: This Schoenhut boy, model #407, was offered undressed in the 1915 catalog only in the 21in (53cm) size and dressed only in the 19in (48cm) size. *Private Collection.* (See page 165 for other Schoenhut dolls.)

A 10in (25cm) hand-carved wood boy made in Switzerland in the early 20th Century. He is peg-jointed with carved shoes and stockings, as well as a carved cap. His costume is original. *H&J Foulke, Inc.* (For another Swiss wooden doll, see page 165.)

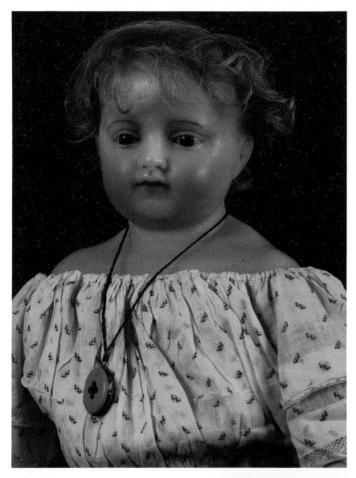

A 24in (61cm) English poured wax child signed by Montanari. The beautiful flesh-colored tones are typical of this family's work. *Private Collection.*

TOP RIGHT: A German wax-over papier-mâché young lady with fancy molded blonde curls and molded red hair bow. She is 23in (58cm) tall. *Joanna Ott Collection.* (For other wax-over dolls, see pages 168 and 177.)

RIGHT: A 17in (43cm) English poured wax baby signed by Pierotti. She still retains her original clothing. The fair number of these babies that have survived with elaborate original clothing indicates that many of them might not have been played with, but rather simply displayed. *Joanna Ott Collection.* (For other poured wax dolls, see pages 166 and 167.)

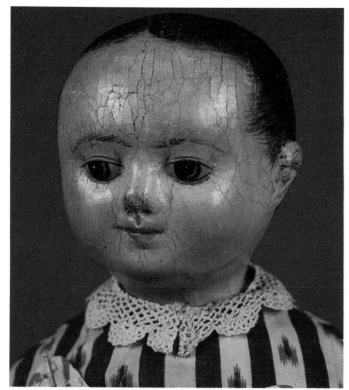

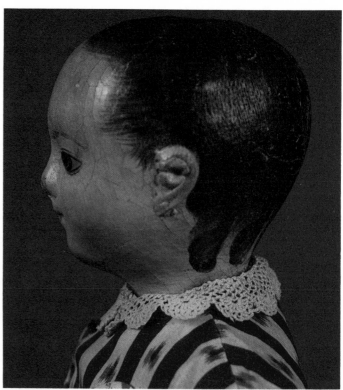

A beautiful American doll by Izannah Walker, very much in demand by collectors and considered to be the most desirable American cloth doll. Izannah Walker patented her dolls in 1873, but was probably making dolls like the one pictured as early as 1840. The doll has an interesting molded and sewn ear. Her brown hair is painted with long curls across the back of her neck and brush strokes at her temples to give the look of individual strands of hair. She is 18in (46cm) tall. *Private Collection.*

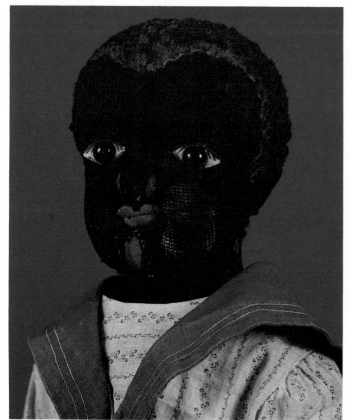

A very interesting 20in (51cm) black cloth doll made of stockinette. He has inset black bead eyes with upper eyelashes and a red yarn mouth. *Private Collection.*

Louise Kampes made cloth dolls with molded and painted faces during the 1920s. She was located in Atlantic City, New Jersey, on the boardwalk. The *Kamkins* dolls' faces all seem to be from the same mold. The dolls have soft, natural looking bobbed mohair wigs. The dolls and clothes were made by home workers. This 19in (48cm) *Kamkins* is all original. *Private Collection.*

"Babyland Rag Dolls" was a trademark of E.I. Horsman in New York for a line of dolls introduced in 1904. The early dolls had hand-painted faces, but in 1907 the printed "lifelike" faces were introduced. Dolls are all unmarked. This *Babyland Rag* doll with black hand-painted face, black mohair wig and original clothing dates from 1904. *H&J Foulke, Inc.*

An early 1915 *Raggedy Ann* and companion *Raggedy Andy*. They are in original clothing although *Ann* has lost her apron. *Jan Foulke Collection.* (For a later pair of *Raggedys*, see page 182.)

This 14in (36cm) cloth doll by Steiff appears to be *Schneid the Tailor* from the artisan series in the 1913 Steiff catalog which also included a butcher and shoemaker. He is wearing his original clothing. His hair and mustache are of inset mohair and he has black button eyes. *Nancy Smith Collection.*

A 17in (43cm) *Fire Brigade Commander* from Steiff's 1913 catalog. This caricature has a prominent proboscis and inset mohair to form sideburns. His original brass helmet has a red tassel and leather strap. *Nancy Smith Collection.* (For another Steiff doll, see page 183.)

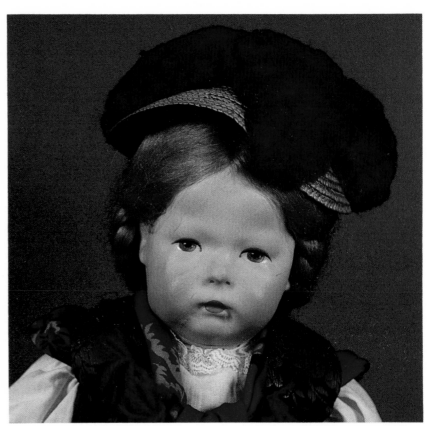

This 17in (43cm) cloth child by Käthe Kruse is an example of Doll IH, the "H" meaning she has a wig and dates after 1929. She is wearing an original German regional costume. *Rosemary Dent Collection.* (For other Käthe Kruse dolls, see pages 183 to 185.)

A very unusual Lenci doll made in a sitting position with curved limbs and unusual character face. She is shown in the 1925/26 Lenci Catalog as 178/G. *Beth Foulke Collection.* (For other Lenci dolls, see pages 185 and 186.)

Two very colorful Italian made dolls showing the Lenci influence. They are unmarked, but very good quality. *H&J Foulke, Inc.*

Alexander Doll Co. released *Wendy-Ann* in 1936. She was a unique doll in that she had a swivel waist so that she could bend and turn. This special waist was made only in the 14in (36cm) size. This *Wendy-Ann* with dark brown human hair wig is wearing a tagged original outfit. *H&J Foulke, Inc.*

TOP RIGHT: Alexander Doll Co. *Fairy Queen* from 1942 in all original outfit, 18in (46cm) tall. *H&J Foulke, Inc.* (For more information about Alexander composition dolls, see pages 191 and 198.)

RIGHT: This Alexander Doll Co. *Bride* from the 1940s is all original. She is 14in (36cm) tall. *H&J Foulke, Inc.*

Probably the first big doll hit of the Alexander Doll Co. was the *Dionne Quintuplets* which were made in a variety of types and sizes beginning in 1935. This 12in (31cm) all-composition toddler is all original with her gold-colored name pin. She is unusual in that she has molded hair and open mouth. Her pink dress means that she is *Yvonne. H&J Foulke, Inc.*

TOP LEFT: Alexander Doll Co. *Doctor* doll which was designed in 1936 to be "Dr. Dafoe," the doctor for the Dionne Quintuplets. He is 14in (36cm) tall in original tagged white doctor's outfit. He has a very interesting character face with gray mohair wig and painted eyes. *India Stoessel Collection.*

LEFT: This beautiful Effanbee doll is one of their *Historical Doll Replicas* which were issued in 1939 as a series of 30 dolls to portray the history of American fashion 1492-1939. These 14in (36cm) dolls used the *Anne Shirley* face with painted eyes and individually designed and fashioned wigs. This doll is representative of United States fashion in 1750. *Rosemary Dent Collection.*

Continued from page 168.

CLOCKWISE: Illustration 318. Fritz Bartenstein patented his double-faced doll in 1880. The head is encased in a permanent hood and rotates on a vertical axis when a string is pulled. The doll also cries "Mama" when the head is turned. The double-faced wax-over-composition doll is showing her pouty or crying face. She is 15in (38cm) tall. *Emily Manning Collection.*

Illustration 319. Another Fritz Bartenstein patent doll with original cap and shift. She is showing her smiling face. *Elizabeth Kennedy Collection.*

Illustration 320. A very unusual wax-over papier-mâché lady with molded plumed hat and mohair curls. She has pierced ears and bulgy glass eyes. Her shoulder head is attached to a cloth body with wooden arms. She is 12in (31cm) tall. *Private Collection.*

VIII. Cloth Dolls

Cloth dolls were undoubtedly made as home projects throughout recorded history. Most surviving examples of homemade and primitive-type cloth dolls date from the 1800s. With the country look so popular in modern home decorating, these primitive American cloth dolls are experiencing a period of great popularity and high prices. As with a work of art, the evaluation of these handmade dolls is purely subjective and based wholly upon appearance, observation of many examples, and "gut feeling" in the observer as to whether or not the doll has a "strong presence" or makes a "strong statement."

Although there are earlier examples extant dating back to the 1600s, very few of these early cloth dolls have survived because of the heavy toll that atmospheric conditions, light and insects take on cloth.

Undoubtedly, there were some early commercial ventures in cloth dolls, but little has been discovered about these. Cloth dolls, as they are generally known in the doll world, were a fairly late development, not much before the third quarter of the 19th Century. A few pressed and molded cloth shoulder head dolls resembling china heads in looks date from the mid 1800s but are of unknown origins. The American George Hawkins of New York made pressed cloth shoulder heads, but most of these are used on his toys and not for play dolls. The American Izannah Walker appears to be one of the first to have commercially produced cloth dolls which she patented in 1873, but probably was producing as early as the 1840s. (See photograph on page 172.) By the turn of the century, Martha Chase was manufacturing cloth dolls, J.B. Shephard of Philadelphia was offering his *Philadelphia Babies* and Horsman was offering the *Babyland Rag* dolls.

Margarete Steiff appears to be one of the first European makers to offer cloth dolls, as early as 1893, although her production of cloth dolls did not peak until after 1900. Käthe Kruse appeared on the scene along in about 1910 with her line which was very popular. It was the tremendous success of the Italian Art Dolls manufactured by Lenci in 1921, however, that started a cloth doll craze and hundreds of companies began producing molded cloth dolls.

A. American Cloth Dolls

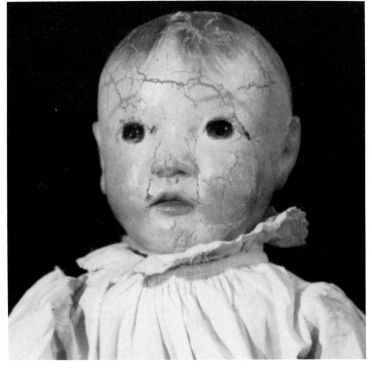

Illustration 321. J. B. Sheppard & Co. in Philadelphia, Pennsylvania, distributed these cloth dolls, popularly called *Philadelphia Babies* by collectors. The features on the painted faces were very well modeled; several different molds are known. Bodies were stockinette and the lower arms and legs were also painted. Dating from about 1900, the dolls were made in sizes 18-22in (46-56cm). *H&J Foulke, Inc.*

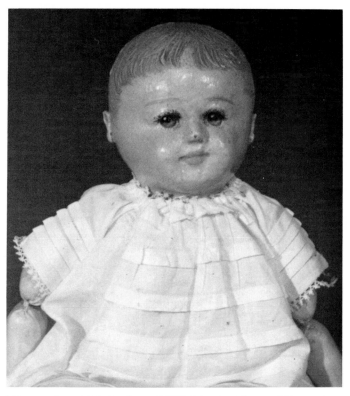

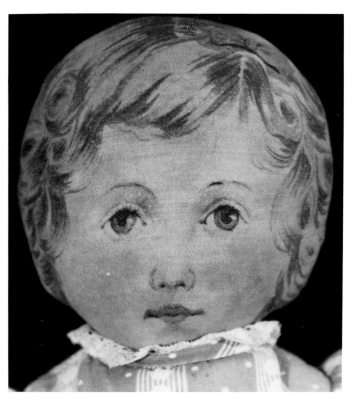

Illustration 322. In about 1889, Martha Chase of Pawtucket, Rhode Island, made cloth dolls with molded head and limbs of stockinette painted with oils. The hair was molded in various styles and rough-stroked to provide texture. The ears are separately applied. Eyes of Chase dolls are brightly painted and highlighted with red eyeline and thick upper eyelashes. Bodies are cloth with seam joints at shoulders, elbows, hips and knees. Later dolls are jointed only at shoulders and hips. Some dolls have completely painted washable bodies; many were designed for use in hospital training. Mrs. Chase made molds for her dolls from bisque doll heads. This very appealing Chase Baby is 17in (43cm) tall. *H&J Foulke, Inc.*

Illustration 323. Dolls which were printed on cloth, cut out and sewn together were cheap and popular for buyers in the early 1900s. These appear to have been American inventions, as they have no European counterparts in the early stages. Apparently, the most popular one is the Art Fabric Mills girl with blonde hair and red hair bow wearing printed red stockings and black boots. Her face is very sweet and appealing. She was patented in 1900. She was made in a variety of sizes from 6in (15cm) to 30in (76cm). *H&J Foulke, Inc.*

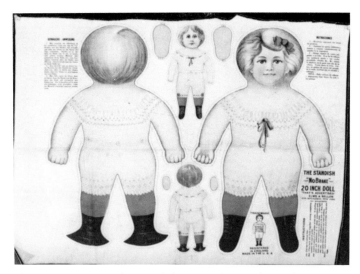

Illustration 324. The *Standish No Break Doll*, dating from 1918, was made by Elms & Sellon Co. A large and small doll came together on one printed sheet. *H&J Foulke, Inc.*

Illustration 325. *Dolly Dear*, designed by book illustrator Frances Brundage, was printed by Saalfield Publishing Co. and copyrighted in 1916. *H&J Foulke, Inc.*

Illustration 326. *Darkey Doll*, patented in 1893, was made by Cocheco Manufacturing Co. It was interesting in that it was designed to have a shaped face, rather than simply flat like other printed-on cloth dolls. *H&J Foulke, Inc.*

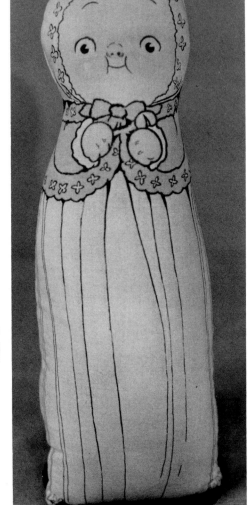

Illustration 327. 13in (33cm) signed G.G. Drayton (Grace) printed-on cloth baby from her "Hug-Me-Tight" line of 1915-1917 made by Colonial Toy Manufacturing Co. *Mother Goose* and other storybook characters were part of this line also. *H&J Foulke, Inc.*

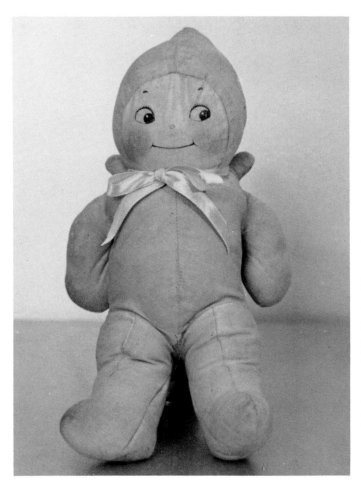

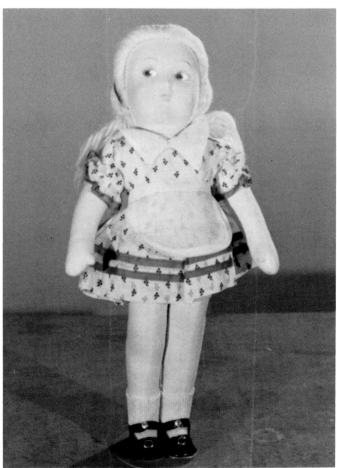

CLOCKWISE: Illustration 328. Rose O'Neill's *Kewpie* dolls came in many materials, including this 12in (31cm) cloth *Cuddle Kewpie* made by Richard G. Kreuger, Inc. of New York, under U.S. Patent #1785800. *Cuddle Kewpie* has a printed mask face and chubby body including tiny shaped wings. *H&J Foulke, Inc.*

Illustration 329. The first dolls made by the now famous Alexander Doll Co. of New York were cloth ones. In the 1930s, Alexander produced a fairly large variety of them, many of which were storybook characters. This doll, *Alice in Wonderland*, appears to be the 1933 version with the plush face. She is all original. *Ann Tardie Collection.*

Illustration 330. The Alexander Co. released their *Little Shavers* dolls in 1942. These were based on the paintings of Elsie Shaver's Victorian children which had been seen by Mme. Alexander at an art exhibition. The *Little Shavers* have cloth mask faces with eyes painted to the side, and pink cloth bodies. Their wigs are of wool yarn. *Ann Tardie Collection.*

Illustration 331. *Raggedy Ann & Andy* are timeless rag dolls designed by Johnny Gruelle and based on his stories about their adventures. Patented in 1915, they are still being made today. This pair made by Molly-'es Doll Outfitters date from 1935-1938. They are all original. *Jan Foulke Collection.* (See color photograph on page 173 for an earlier pair of *Raggedys.*)

B. European Cloth Dolls

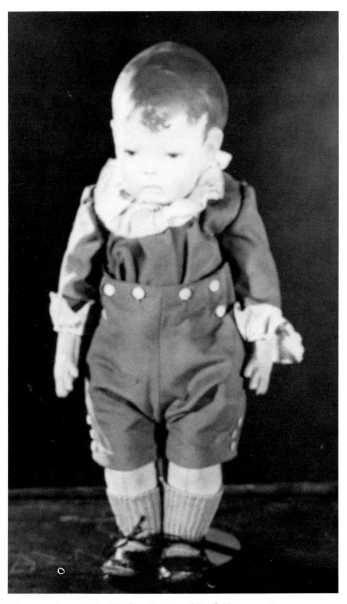

Illustration 332. The Margarete Steiff Company of Giengen began to produce felt dolls in 1893, but it was not until 1904 that they began to use their famous trademark on the dolls, a small metal button in the ear. Steiff called these extremely well constructed felt play dolls "Character Dolls." They have a center face seam to facilitate facial modeling and tiny glass eyes as well as mohair wigs which are an integral part of the dolls. These play dolls were dressed as schoolchildren or in charming regional costumes which were removable. They were available in 28, 36 and 43cm (11, 14 and 17in) sizes. The pictured girl wearing original outfit is 11in (28cm) tall. *Joyce Alderson Collection.* (For color photographs of Steiff comic or caricature dolls, see pages 173 and 174.)

Illustration 333. Käthe Kruse of Bad Kosen, Germany, was important in the German doll reform movement in that her dolls were a real departure from the popular German bisque dolly faces. She first made cloth play dolls for her own daughters. In 1910, she exhibited some of her dolls in Berlin and was an instant success, although producing enough dolls to fulfill the demand was at first a problem. By 1912, her dolls were coming into the United States. The dolls are entirely of cloth with molded and painted hair and faces and swivel hip joints. This example of Doll I in original clothing measures between 16 and 17in (41-43cm), standard size of the first dolls. Käthe Kruse dolls are stamped and numbered on the foot. *H&J Foulke, Inc.* (For a color photograph of a Kruse doll, see page 174.)

OPPOSITE PAGE: **Illustration 334.** In 1929, some of the Series I dolls were given wigs made of human hair which was inset into a wig cap. Series VIII "German Child" which was 20½in (52cm) was introduced. This example of the "German Child" Series VIII is all original. *H&J Foulke, Inc.*

Illustration 336. A 16in (41cm) Lenci girl with face 149. Her wavy mohair wig is made from one long strip of mohair applied in concentric circles on her felt pate. She is dressed in original clothing. *Beth Foulke Collection.*

Illustration 335. Lenci dolls, designed by Elena di Scavini of Turin, Italy, were patented in 1921, although she had started to make them probably as early as 1918. Early Lenci dolls are skillfully fashioned entirely from felt with movable joints. The faces are of pressed and shaped felt, artistically painted with appealing pouty or winsome expressions. An early advertisement claimed "Every Lenci is Made in Italy by Italian Artists and is an individual Work of Art." Lenci dolls were beautifully dressed in colorful, often fanciful and elaborate costumes, usually of felt, sometimes combined with organdy. They were expensive and appealed to the carriage trade. The pictured doll is a 16in (41cm) Lenci girl number 159G, all original with labels and box. *Beth Foulke Collection.*

RIGHT: Illustration 337. This 26in (66cm) Lenci Boudoir Lady doll has a long slender body with high-heeled shoes and fancy-styled blonde mohair wig. Her organdy dress has appliqued decorations and she carries her mirror. *H&J Foulke, Inc.*

185

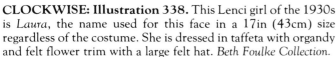

CLOCKWISE: Illustration 338. This Lenci girl of the 1930s is *Laura*, the name used for this face in a 17in (43cm) size regardless of the costume. She is dressed in taffeta with organdy and felt flower trim with a large felt hat. *Beth Foulke Collection.*

Illustration 339. Norah Wellings was a designer for the English Chad Valley firm before she started out on her own in 1926. She is best known for her small felt and velveteen sailors, policemen, Scots, black natives, Indians and others which were sold as souvenir dolls. However, she also made child play dolls, some in very large sizes. This 12in (31cm) girl is all original with her cardboard label. *H&J Foulke, Inc.*

Illustration 340. Another English manufacturer who was making cloth child dolls during this period was J.K. Farnell which used the trademark "Alpha Toys." This 16in (41cm) doll is in her original Scots outfit. *H&J Foulke, Inc.*

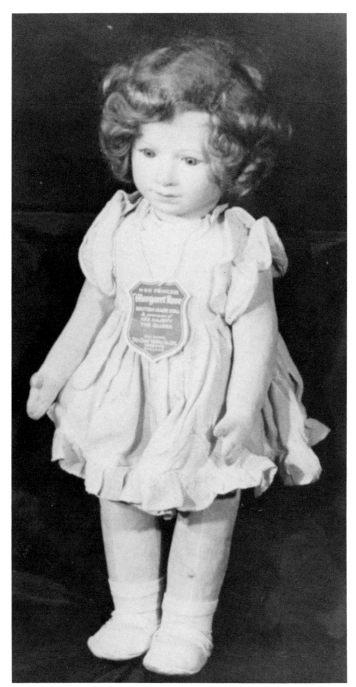

Illustration 342. Bernard Ravca began making dolls in Paris, France, in 1924. After 1939, he moved to the United States. He is known for his marvelous portrait faces of old people needlesculpted from stockinette. These lovely French peasant dolls in original costumes with labels are 10in (25cm) tall. *H&J Foulke, Inc.*

Illustration 341. The English Chad Valley company also made cloth child dolls with felt faces beginning in the mid 1920s. Their most famous dolls, however, are of the Royal Children, Princesses Elizabeth and Margaret Rose which they made in the late 1930s. These dolls usually had glass inset eyes. This example of *Margaret Rose* in her original pink dress is 16in (41cm) tall. *Richard Wright Antiques.*

RIGHT: Illustration 343. A 16in (41cm) all-cloth doll by Eugenie Poir, Paris, France. She has a wavy blonde mohair wig and lovely organdy and felt dress with felt flower trim, obviously another doll showing the Lenci influence. *H&J Foulke, Inc.*

IX. American Composition Dolls

World War I (1914-1919) and the closing of European doll markets to the United States spurred heightened interest among American doll companies to explore new avenues of doll production. Although some doll companies, such as Ideal Novelty & Toy Co., which started to manufacture composition dolls in the early 1900s, E.I. Horsman of New York with composition dolls which started manufacturing in about 1910 and Albert Schoenhut of Philadelphia with wooden dolls in 1911, there was little going on in the United States as far as mass-producing dolls was concerned. There was some cloth doll production by Martha Chase and Horsman distributed cloth dolls, also, but these were hardly enough to fill the great void caused by the cessation of German imports. Although some American potteries, such as Fulper in Flemington, New Jersey, tried manufacturing bisque heads, these met with only limited success.

It was in the development of the unbreakable and durable composition doll by numerous new doll making companies that American efforts finally excelled. Even though European dolls were again available a little after the war ended in 1919, they never did again dominate the American doll market as they had previously. American dolls continued to be strong and by the 1930s, nearly all dolls sold in America were American-made.

A. Celebrities, Personalities and Storybook Dolls

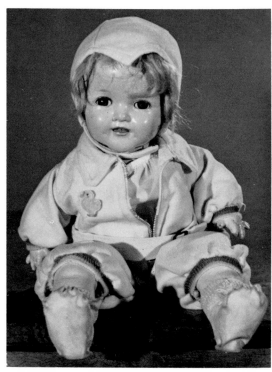

Illustration 344. The authentic and licensed *Shirley Temple* doll made by Ideal Novelty & Toy Co. was probably the biggest doll success that Ideal ever had. Millions of *Shirleys* were sold over a period of 50 years, first in composition and later in vinyl. Composition *Shirley* released in 1934 was made in many sizes ranging from 11in (28cm) to 27in (69cm) and in a wide variety of lovely dresses, some of which were from her movies. This 16in (41cm) composition *Shirley Temple* is a hard-to-find size. She is marked on both head and body and wears a tagged dress with her original button. *H&J Foulke, Inc.*

Illustration 345. In comparison to the number of *Shirley Temple* child dolls, only a relatively few of the *Shirley Temple* baby dolls were made. This 16in (41cm) baby with composition head, arms and legs on cloth body is wearing her original pink labeled snowsuit. *H&J Foulke, Inc.*

Illustration 346. Ideal's *Judy Garland*, which dates from 1939, is here dressed in her blue checked dress as "Dorothy" from *The Wizard of Oz*. This doll in no way reached the popularity of the *Shirley Temple* one, and is today in short supply and great demand. This all-original example is 16in (41cm) tall. *Rosemary Dent Collection.*

Illustration 347. *Deanna Durbin* was put out by Ideal Novelty & Toy Co. in 1938, in sizes ranging from 14-25in (36-64cm). She is wearing her original cotton print gown and metal button with her picture. This example is 21in (53cm) tall. *Rosemary Dent Collection.*

TOP LEFT: Illustration 348. This rare version of *Deanna Durbin* by Ideal shows her as "Gulliver." This doll has a jet black mohair wig, deeper face coloring, brown sleeping eyes (although some with this outfit have painted eyes), and feathered eyebrows. She is 21in (53cm) tall. *Rosemary Dent Collection.*

TOP RIGHT: Illustration 349. Snow White was all the rage in 1938, and as a tie-in with the new Walt Disney film, *Snow White and the Seven Dwarfs*, dominated the advertisements in the toy trade journals. Ideal was one of the companies licensed to produce *Snow White* dolls. Ideal used the *Shirley Temple* body for their doll. Her original dress identifies her as "Snow White" and has line drawings of the "Seven Dwarfs" around the bottom of the skirt. The pictured doll is 18in (46cm) tall, although sometimes a smaller size doll is found. *H&J Foulke, Inc.*

RIGHT: Illustration 350. *Baby Sandy* was a movie star doll made by Ralph Freundlich from 1939-1942. This chubby toddler doll has a cute, smiling face just like the real "Baby Sandy Henville." She is 16in (41cm) tall, wearing her original blue organdy dress with metal button. *Rosemary Dent Collection.*

Illustration 351. *Princess Elizabeth* was designed by Madame Alexander for the May 12, 1937, coronation of her father, George VI, King of England. She was a sure success, as everyone is interested in real princesses and every little girl at some time or another likes to imagine herself one. *Princess Elizabeth* generally is dressed in a gown and tiara. This example is 16in (41cm) tall. *Mary Lou Rubright Collection.*

B. Child Dolls

Illustration 352. The *Campbell Kids*, which Grace Drayton designed for the Campbell Soup Co., were manufactured by the E.I. Horsman Co. beginning in 1910. The heads and usually the hands were of Horsman's tough "Can't Break 'Em" composition while the bodies were hard stuffed cloth. These 9in (23cm) and 13in (33cm) *Campbell Kids* are all original with a cloth tag on their sleeves. They came in a wide range of clothing as boys or girls, some with wigs. *Richard Wright Collection.*

RIGHT: Illustration 353. By 1928, the *Campbell Kids* were being made by American Character Doll Co. under their "Petite" trademark. These dolls were 12in (31cm) tall and were all-composition with a variety of cute dresses. Sometimes collectors refer to this doll as *Dolly Dingle* as it is also a Grace Drayton design. *Maxine Salaman Collection.*

CLOCKWISE: **Illustration 354.** By 1947, E.I. Horsman was again making *Campbell Kids* from a new design, all of composition with molded and painted shoes and stockings. The dolls were 12in (31cm) tall and came as either boy or girl models, some in matching pairs. *Maxine Salaman Collection.*

Illustration 355. In 1927, Grace Corry designed this head for Averill Manufacturing Co. (Madame Hendren). The sweet smiling faces are very appealing and were called *Little Brother* and *Little Sister.* The dolls came in a variety of outfits as little children, storybook characters or in regional costumes. These 15in (38cm) dolls are in tagged Madame Hendren felt Dutch costumes. *H&J Foulke, Inc.*

Illustration 356. American Character Doll Co. produced the *Puggy* doll in 1928. He is all-composition with a wonderful scowling character face, 12in (31cm) tall. *Becky Roberts Lowe.*

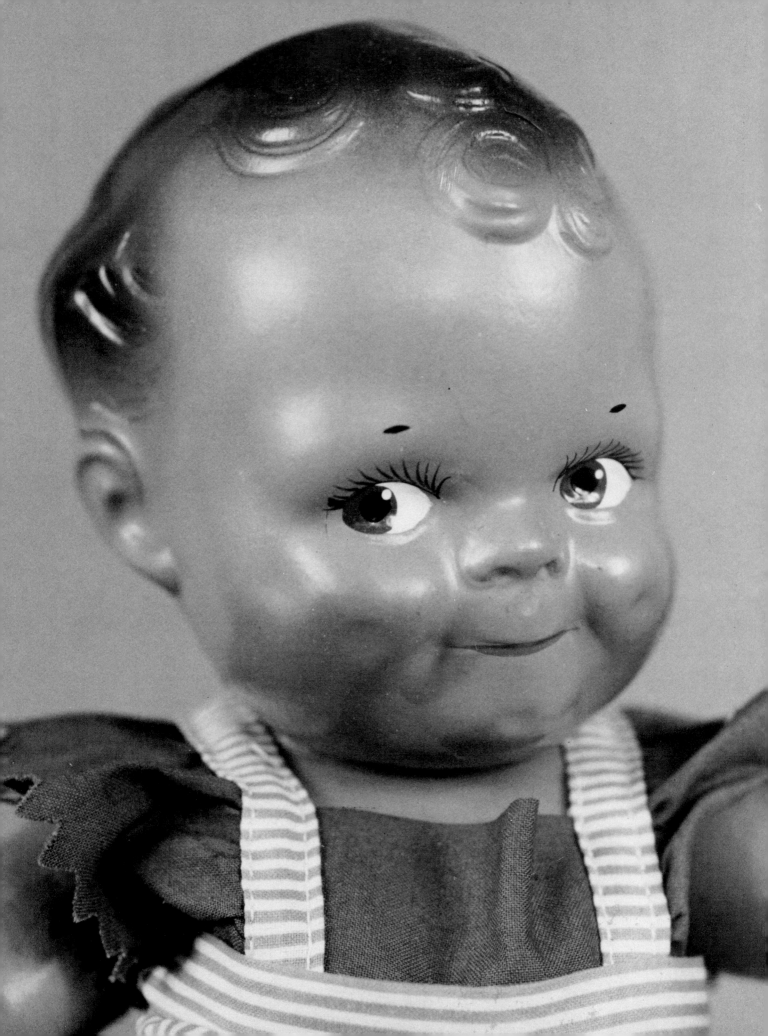

OPPOSITE PAGE: Illustration 357. If Rose O'Neill's most famous doll was *Kewpie* (see *Illustrations 247* and *248*), *Scootles* designed in 1925 probably came in second. The doll is all-composition with molded hair and impish smile. The illustrated doll is shown in a rare brown-skinned version in a 14in (36cm) size. *H&J Foulke, Inc.*

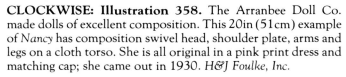

CLOCKWISE: Illustration 358. The Arranbee Doll Co. made dolls of excellent composition. This 20in (51cm) example of *Nancy* has composition swivel head, shoulder plate, arms and legs on a cloth torso. She is all original in a pink print dress and matching cap; she came out in 1930. *H&J Foulke, Inc.*

Illustration 359. Some of the most beautiful composition dolls were produced by Madame Alexander. The composition was of excellent quality; the wigs were individually styled for different dolls; the clothing was constructed with much attention to detail. *McGuffey Ana*, the little schoolgirl named after the old-fashioned *McGuffey Readers*, issued in 1937, was a very popular model. She came in every size from 9in (23cm) to 24in (61cm). This 20in (51cm) doll is all original. *H&J Foulke, Inc.*

Illustration 360. The most realistic and lifelike composition dolls ever manufactured were those designed by Dewees Cochran and produced by Effanbee Doll Co. They were called "American Children" and came out in 1939. This 19in (48cm) *Peggy Lou* is all original. Her beautiful face has painted eyes, multi-stroked eyebrows and an expressive mouth. *Maxine Salaman Collection.*

Illustration 361. A 17in (43cm) boy was part of the "American Children" series produced by the Effanbee Doll Co. and designed by Dewees Cochran. The doll is all-composition with painted eyes and closed, almost smiling mouth. He is very difficult to find. The pictured doll is all original. *H&J Foulke, Inc.*

BELOW: Illustration 362. *Patsy,* "The Lovable Imp with tiltable head and movable limb" created by Bernard Lipfert for Effanbee Doll Co. first appeared in 1927. *Patsy* had stylish molded bobbed hair and was completely made of excellent quality composition with painted eyes. (Later *Patsys* had wigs and sleeping eyes.) *Patsy* and her relatives were enormously popular and must have been manufactured by the millions. She was undoubtedly one of Effanbee's greatest successes. *Patsy* is always 14in (36cm) tall. The pictured doll has on original playsuit, shoes, stockings and hair bow. *H&J Foulke, Inc.*

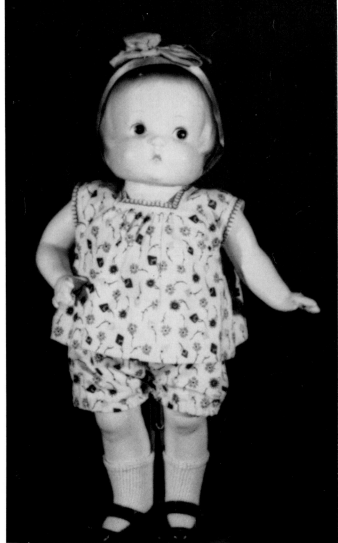

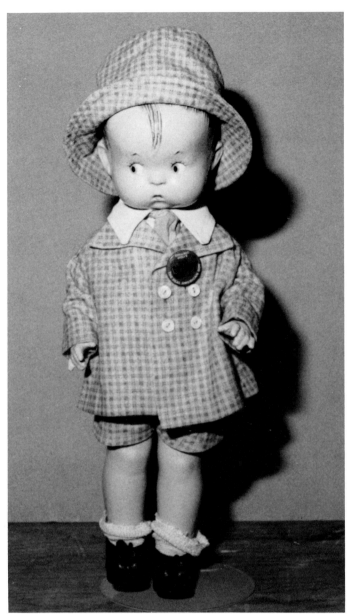

CLOCKWISE: Illustration 363. In 1929, Effanbee was advertising *Skippy* as "Patsy's Boy Friend." *Skippy* was from the comic strip created by Percy Crosby. He has molded hair and an impish, yet wistful look with very full cheeks and side-glancing eyes. Also 14in (36cm) tall, at first he was on a *Patsy* body, later on a cloth body with composition arms and legs with molded over-the-knee boots. The pictured *Skippy* is in original costume. *Glenn Mandeville/Chip Barkel Collection.*

Illustration 364. Effanbee put out 26in (66cm) tall *Patsy Ruth* in the mid 1930s. She has a human hair wig and lashed sleeping eyes. Apparently, only a few of this doll were made as she is very difficult to find. The pictured doll is shown in original clothing. *Maxine Salaman Collection.*

Illustration 365. *Rosemary* was Effanbee's Christmas doll for 1925 and according to their advertising was "the darling doll that won't wear out." She was a toddler doll with composition shoulder head, chubby arms and legs with a cloth torso. The pictured *Rosemary* is 14in (36cm), although she came in sizes up to 26in (66cm). She is shown in her original clothing. *H&J Foulke, Inc.*

C. Lady and Teenage Dolls

CLOCKWISE: Illustration 366. Brides and bridesmaids have always been included in the Alexander Doll Co. line. They were especially popular in the mid 1940s when whole bridal parties were available. The composition *Wendy-Ann* face used on the bridal dolls was first released in 1936 or 1937. The pictured bridesmaid is wearing a blue satin gown with flower ornament in her blonde mohair wig. She is 21 in (53cm) tall. *H&J Foulke, Inc.* (For color photographs of other Alexander composition dolls with the *Wendy-Ann* face, see page 175.)

Illustration 367. Mme. Alexander designed the *Margaret* face for a *Margaret O'Brien* doll which was made in composition from 1946-1947. Of course, the face was used for other dolls as well, including a doll considered by many collectors to be one of Alexander's most beautiful models, *Karen Ballerina* of 1946. Her dress is pink net with gold trim. Her hair is lovely blonde floss arranged in coiled braids with pink flowers entwined. This particular doll is 21 in (53cm) tall. *H&J Foulke, Inc.*

Illustration 368. Effanbee Doll Co.'s popular doll of the 1940s was *Little Lady* which was really an extension of the *Anne Shirley* line as the doll had the same face and body with the lovely arms with separate fingers designed by Dewees Cochran for the "American Children" dolls. The doll was sometimes dressed in schoolgirl clothing, sometimes as a grown-up. Here is *Little Lady* at 17 in (43cm) tall dressed in a fancy organdy gown with layers of ruffles. These dolls are made of excellent quality composition. *H&J Foulke, Inc.*

Illustration 369. A very rare Effanbee composition doll is this 6in (15cm) one, all original and boxed with her wrist tag. The doll appears to be the same as *Wee Patsy* with an added mohair wig. It has molded shoes and stockings. It could possibly be one of a series of small portrait or storybook dolls, but no others have turned up to date. *H&J Foulke, Inc.*

RIGHT: Illustration 370. In 1940, Effanbee manufactured a series of 11in (28cm) "Portrait Dolls." This is the *Gibson Girl* doll from that series. Others included a ballerina, bride and groom, Spanish dancing couple and colonial lady. *H&J Foulke, Inc.*

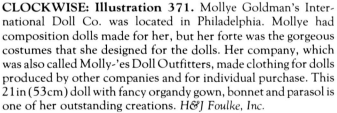

CLOCKWISE: Illustration 371. Mollye Goldman's International Doll Co. was located in Philadelphia. Mollye had composition dolls made for her, but her forte was the gorgeous costumes that she designed for the dolls. Her company, which was also called Molly-'es Doll Outfitters, made clothing for dolls produced by other companies and for individual purchase. This 21in (53cm) doll with fancy organdy gown, bonnet and parasol is one of her outstanding creations. *H&J Foulke, Inc.*

Illustration 372. Monica Doll Studios of Hollywood, California, produced a composition doll in the 1940s which was unique because it had human hair rooted in the scalp. The pictured *Monica* doll is 21in (53cm) tall. *H&J Foulke, Inc.*

Illustration 373. Arranbee Doll Co. produced their *Debu' Teen* doll beginning in 1938. In this 14in (36cm) size, she is very similar if not exactly like the *Mary Hoyer* doll. The Arranbee dolls are known for their good quality composition. *Maxine Salaman Collection.*

D. Baby Dolls

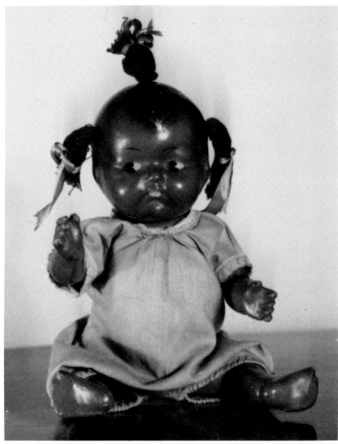

CLOCKWISE: Illustration 374. This is a yellow composition *Ming Ming Baby* made by Quan-Quan Co., Los Angeles and San Francisco, California, in the 1930s. These Oriental babies are dressed in beautifully made costumes of satin and braid. He is 12in (31cm) tall. *H&J Foulke, Inc.*

Illustration 375. A popular baby of the 1930s and 1940s made by a variety of companies is the black composition *Topsy* doll with three black braids coming through holes drilled in her head. Sizes generally ran from 9-12in (23-31cm) and the dolls generally wore some type of inexpensive playsuit. This baby is marked "G E W." *Private Collection.*

Illustration 376. Effanbee Doll Co.'s *Lovums* with its happy smiling face was a popular doll for at least ten years, beginning in 1928. *Lovums* was a mama doll with a soft cloth body and composition arms and legs. Effanbee dolls were known for high quality composition as well as well-designed and made clothing. This 16in (41cm) *Lovums* is dressed in fancy organdy and lace-trimmed dress and bonnet. *H&J Foulke, Inc.*

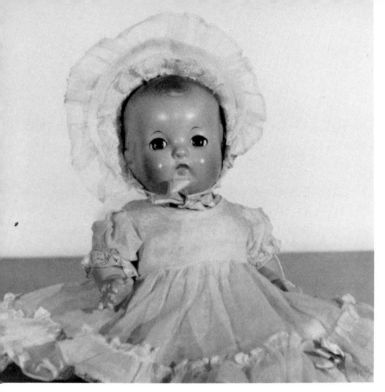

Illustration 377. The Effanbee Doll Co. introduced several babies as part of the *Patsy* family line. *Patsy Babyette* came out in 1927. She is 8in (20cm) tall and dressed here in a fancy organdy baby dress and matching hat. Some of these dolls were dressed as boy and girl twins. *H&J Foulke, Inc.*

RIGHT: Illustration 378. One of Effanbee Doll Co.'s cutest babies is this baby which in this overall outfit was marketed as *Tommy Tucker.* He has a composition head with flirty eyes which move from side to side as he is moved. He has a soft cloth body with composition hands. This face in different clothing was also marketed as *Mickey, Baby Bright Eyes* and *Sweetie Pie.* The pictured doll is 16in (41cm) tall. *Glenn Mandeville/Chip Barkel Collection.*

Illustrations 379, 380 and 381. *Trudy* was designed by Elsie Gilbert and made by the Three-in-One Doll Corp. of New York in 1946. She was offered in the 1949 Sears, Roebuck and Co. catalog for $4.79 wearing a cotton dress and bonnet. More often *Trudy* is found in her pink plush sleeper as pictured. She is 14in (36cm) tall. *H&J Foulke, Inc.*

E. Novelty Dolls

TOP LEFT: Illustration 382. E.I. Horsman produced many novelty dolls. A cute series from 1916 was the *Gene Carr Kids* dolls designed by Bernard Lipfert from Gene Carr's cartoon characters. The dolls were 14in (36cm) tall and included wide-eyed *Mike* and *Jane* as well as *Snowball* (black), and *Blink* and *Skinney*, both with eyes closed. *Mike* has reddish painted hair and a grinning mischievous face. *H&J Foulke, Inc.*

LEFT: Illustration 383. *Betty Boop* was designed by J.L. Kallus and made by the Cameo Doll Co. with permission of Fleischer Studios. She usually is found with molded bathing suit torso and wood segmented legs, but this is the rarer model with composition torso (labeled) and composition legs. She is 12in (31cm) tall. *Richard Wright Collection.*

TOP RIGHT: Illustration 384. The maker of this 20in (51cm) all-composition *Santa Claus* doll is unknown, but it appears to be American. The head is beautifully modeled with red cap and white whiskers, hair and mustache. It is a difficult doll to find. *Mary Lou Rubright Collection.*

Bibliography

Angione, Genevieve. *All-Bisque & Half-Bisque Dolls.* Exton, Pennsylvania: Schiffer Publishing Ltd., 1969.

Borger, Mona. *Chinas, Dolls for Study and Admiration.* San Francisco: Borger Publications, 1983.

Cieslik, Jürgen and Marianne. *German Doll Encyclopedia, 1800-1939.* Cumberland, Maryland: Hobby House Press, Inc., 1985.

Coleman, Dorothy S., Elizabeth Ann, and Evelyn Jane. *The Collector's Book of Dolls' Clothes, Costumes in Miniature: 1700-1929.* New York: Crown Publishers, Inc., 1975.

_____. *The Collector's Encyclopedia of Dolls.* New York: Crown Publishers, Inc., 1968.

_____. *The Collector's Encyclopedia of Dolls, Vol. II.* New York: Crown Publishers, Inc., 1986.

Foulke, Jan. *Focusing on Effanbee Composition Dolls.* Riverdale, Maryland: Hobby House Press, 1978.

_____. *Focusing on Gebrüder Heubach Dolls.* Cumberland, Maryland: Hobby House Press, 1980.

_____. *Kestner, King of Dollmakers.* Cumberland, Maryland: Hobby House Press, Inc., 1982.

_____. *Simon & Halbig Dolls, The Artful Aspect.* Cumberland, Maryland: Hobby House Press, Inc., 1984.

_____. *Treasury of Madame Alexander Dolls.* Riverdale, Maryland: Hobby House Press, 1979.

Gerken, Jo Elizabeth. *Wonderful Dolls of Papier-Mâché.* Lincoln, Nebraska: Doll Research Associates, Union College Press, 1970.

Hillier, Mary. *The History of Wax Dolls.* Cumberland, Maryland: Hobby House Press, Inc., 1985.

Mathes, Ruth E. & R. C. "The Decline & Fall of the Wooden Doll." *Doll Collectors Manual.* Boston: Doll Collectors of America, Inc., 1964.

Merrill, Madeline O. *The Art of Dolls, 1700-1940.* Cumberland, Maryland: Hobby House Press, Inc., 1985.

Tarnowska, Marie. *Fashion Dolls.* Cumberland, Maryland: Hobby House Press, Inc., 1986.

Index

Mark and Mold Numbers